Berlitz

Beijing

Front cover and right: Imperial guardian
lions are a regular fixture in Beijing

TOP 10 ATTRACTIONS

The Temple of Heaven • This temple is located amid a lovely park, where musicians play traditional instruments *(page 46)*

Beihai Park • Historical buildings and pretty lakes feature in this park *(page 3*

The Great Wall • Near the city are restored sections of China's magnificent monument *(page 68)*

The Summer Palace • Temples, pavilions, gardens and lakes abound at this imperial playground *(page 60)*

The Lama Temple • Dating from 1694, this is an ornate – and thriving – place of Tibetan Buddhist worship *(page 41)*

The Panjiayuan Market • A vast assortment of antiques and bric-a-brac *(page 49)*

The White Cloud Temple • The temple's monks practise the indigenous religion of Daoism *(page 54)*

Tiananmen Square • The world's largest urban space, with Jianlou (Arrow Tower) at its southern end *(page 30)*

Chengde • This imperial resort makes a fascinating excursion *(page 78)*

The Forbidden City • Located at the heart of Beijing, it is one of the world's best-preserved historical sights *(page 26)*

CONTENTS

80

74

46

29

105

27

INTRODUCTION

Situated at the northern apex of the North China Plain, Beijing is the most visited of all Chinese cities. As the primary residence for three major dynasties, Beijing has amassed a vast array of imperial treasures. The Forbidden City, where the emperors resided from 1420 to 1924, remains intact, and the best-preserved portions of the Great Wall still guard the city's northern approach. Inheriting the best of Chinese history and art, Beijing protected these treasures during the deaths of dynasties and the throes of revolutions.

Chinese dragon masks at Beijing's Panjiayuan Market

Now, as the capital of a new China, the city can present them to the world as the relics of Old Cathay.

Crossing the vast courtyards of Beijing's palaces and pavilions, you can almost hear the heart of the Middle Kingdom beating. As you peer into the recesses of tile-roofed halls, you can imagine the emperors rising from the Dragon Throne. For five centuries this was the home of China's most powerful dynasties, including the Ming and the Manchu. China's last emperor abandoned the Forbidden City early in the 20th century. But the imperial walls have survived, as have the palaces of the 'Great Within'.

The ancient parks of China's capital have also survived. The Temple of Heaven, where emperors performed the

Silhouette of the iconic Hall of Prayer for Good Harvests

annual rites to ensure the prosperity of the Earth, still stands at the southern end of the Imperial Way in Beijing. The royal processions from the Forbidden City no longer travel along the main axis of the old capital, but thousands of tourists do.

The Summer Palace, formerly a lakeside resort reserved for the imperial court and the private playground of the notorious Empress Dowager Cixi during the twilight of the last dynasty, has endured, to the delight of modern visitors. The once-exclusive shores of the Back Lakes and of Beihai Park, just north of the Forbidden City, are also open for our pleasure today. Dotted with temples, pagodas, imperial altars, classical gardens and ageing mansions, the lakes and parks of old Beijing provide pathways into China's past – a world apart from anything that has ever existed in the West.

A view of ancient Beijing from Jingshan Park

Blending East and West

While Beijing's chief attractions are these exotic monuments to the past, such dazzling surfaces are but one aspect of the Beijing experience. Modern Beijing exerts its own appeal: its streets hold a fascination that is distinctly Chinese. Beijing is famous for its courtyard houses in tiny alleys (hutong) that have changed very little since the Qing Dynasty. In Beijing's hutong neighbourhoods – and on its busiest shopping avenues – East and West engage in a tug of war on every corner. Fortune-tellers haunt the doorsteps of the latest European boutiques and itinerant vendors hawk baked yams at the entrance to Western fast-food outlets.

The capital is still the best place in China to see a performance of the centuries-old Beijing Opera or to feast on a banquet of authentic Beijing duck, but you can also shop at a mega-mall here and travel in a subway.

Modern sculpture and architecture in Eastern Beijing

What most surprises first-time visitors is the capital's modern appearance. China's greatest city is flat, sprawling and unattractive, dominated by monotonous rows of concrete highrise hulks, modelled on the Soviet Union's architecture of 'socialist realism'. However, the most recent phase of construction follows the steel-and-glass skyscraper school of modern city skylines.

At first glance, Beijing looks like an ugly duckling of ultra-modern hotel towers, ageing tenements and massive construction zones encircled by traffic-clogged elevated expressways. This is partly the result of Beijing's sudden economic boom, leaping from a poor, pre-industrial metropolis to the heights of a major world capital and becoming the administrative centre of the largest consumer market in the world.

Since the 1990s, Beijing has pulled out all the stops. But it retains significant sections of its pre-industrial districts, its ancient parks and its imperial monuments. Old Beijing has not been reconstructed out of existence – at least not yet.

Two generations of Beijingers

The Beijingers

The Beijingers themselves are extremely proud of the old capital but not nearly as sentimental about their past glories as outsiders are. They support unfettered progress, rapid modernisation and willy-nilly Westernisation because these volatile processes are eliminating centuries of severe poverty. The old courtyard houses in twisting alleyways might be picturesque, representatives of a profound Beijing tradition, but new apartment towers promise decent living space and comforts previously enjoyed only by emperors. Beijingers are warm and outgoing but frank enough to tell visitors that material progress for their families takes precedence over an emperor's silk robe, a decaying shrine or even the air quality.

Over 17 million people now live in the greater Beijing metropolitan area, with 7.5 million packed within the city limits. This makes Beijing one of the world's largest cities. It is quite crowded in the streets, there's a severe housing shortage and the per-capita income is about US$2,700 a year; the minimum wage is just US$70 a month. Beggars huddle around temples and tourist sites. Beijing's large 'floating population' – consisting of those who arrive from the countryside illegally in the hope of finding work – circulates in the streets.

Yet Beijingers are regarded as extremely prosperous within China, far better off than those on the farms or in other cities lying inland. In fact, there is a rising middle class made up of the well-educated and those who succeed in free enterprises. Most Beijingers are exceptionally optimistic about their prospects.

Beijing is also one of the few cities in China with an international flavour. It has long been the primary host of foreign delegations. In recent decades, Beijing has welcomed from abroad more diplomats, scholars, experts, artists, business travellers and tourists than any other Chinese city. A significant number of Beijing residents are foreign-born, employed by overseas businesses and agencies. It also contains China's leading universities and governmental agencies.

Little Emperors?

Since the one-child policy was introduced in 1979, a single child often has a monopoly over two parents and four doting grandparents. Boys, seen as inheritors of the family line, are spoilt more. Memories of hard times, and the desire to get the most out of one offspring, mean many parents believe bigger is better. Obesity has become common among urban children puffed up by Western fast food and countless brands of snacks and sweets.

In return for this attention, the 'little emperors' face increasing pressure to succeed in their exams. Yet sympathy is in short supply: 'Many of them are selfish, lazy, arrogant and uncaring', wrote *China Daily*.

The Olympic National Stadium, nicknamed the 'Bird's Nest'

A Distinctive Culture

The curious thing is Beijing's essential otherness. Despite its Western appearance, despite its international politics, despite its dedication to Western business practices and free enterprise, and despite its admiration for fast food, imported movies, new cars and personal computers, Beijing is at heart a fully Chinese city, with its own ways of doing things.

Beijing has its own language and cuisine, both of which give it an exotic feel. Travellers who restrict themselves to hotels, tour buses, hired guides and major shops and restaurants will encounter few language problems in Beijing. But everywhere else throughout the city, the sounds and signs are all Chinese. Beijingers speak a local dialect, which happily for them is very close to the official dialect, known as *putonghua* (Mandarin). The rulers in Beijing, of course, were the ones who determined just which of the many varying regional dialects of spoken Chinese became the official version.

Chinese food is more familiar to outsiders than is the Chinese language, but the cuisine of Beijing is also quite distinctive. The flavours are those of North China, seldom resembling the Westernised Cantonese fare of Chinese restaurants in North America and Europe. Chopsticks are the common way to consume a meal, although Western tableware is becoming widely available. The food and the language are both alien elements but must be counted as attractions rather than as obstacles. In Beijing, these and other cultural differences remain solidly in place, along with customs that Western contact and modernisation have not erased.

A multitude of historic sights, scenic parks, old neighbourhoods and ancient temples are scattered throughout modern Beijing. For sightseeing today, buses, taxis, the subway or a rented bike have become necessities. Getting around town can be tedious, and traffic jams are common. The heart of the city is still where it's always been: at the Forbidden City, directly across Chang'an Avenue from Tiananmen Square, the largest public square in the world. The Temple of Heaven is to the south, the Summer Palace to the northwest, and the Great Wall looms to the north. The city retains the chessboard layout with which it was endowed by its Ming emperors.

Traditional music in the Temple of Eternal Peace, Beihai Park

While Beijing is China's top imperial treasurehouse, it is a city undergoing massive reconstruction, sometimes with little regard to preserving its splendid past. Preparations for the 2008 Olympic Games added further urgency to this process of reinvention, although the renovation of major museums and the restoration of historic attractions are also part of the action plan. If you want to see China from two intense perspectives – that of its graceful past and its frenetic future – Beijing lies at a striking point of intersection.

A BRIEF HISTORY

Beijing has often been at the centre of Chinese history, from the rise and fall of dynasties to the recent triumphs and tragedies at Tiananmen Square. Each great phase left visible marks on Beijing, and the capital is a virtual museum devoted to the world's oldest continuous civilisation.

Peking Man

The skull and bones of China's oldest prehistoric resident, Peking Man, were discovered 50km (30 miles) southwest of Beijing in 1929. This excavation at Zhoukoudian, estimated to be 500,000–690,000 years old, constituted a major chapter in modern palaeontology, since it was the first evidence that early man (Homo erectus) might have evolved in Asia as well as Africa.

Visiting Peking Man

The Peking Man Caves and Museum at Zhoukoudian are still a major Beijing tourist site (see page 75), although many of the important fossils are in collections outside China.

In 1996, a Stone Age village, barely 1km (half a mile) from the Forbidden City and Tiananmen Square, was discovered. The stone implements and human fossils at this site, beneath the new Oriental Plaza complex, are now on public view in a basement gallery. They push the known human settlement of central Beijing back to 20,000BC.

Capital of the Khans

There are records of a town existing at Beijing as early as the Western Zhou Dynasty (1100–771BC), but the growth of the city did not begin until the end of the Tang Dynasty (AD618–907). Invaders from the north, the Khitan, swept down and made Beijing their secondary capital, from which they controlled much of northern China. This period was known as the Liao Dynasty (AD916–1125), but there are almost no traces of it in Beijing today. The Liao capital at Beijing, then known as Yanjing, occupied the southeast region of what is the modern capital today, with the Fayuan Temple the only surviving monument.

Another swarm of nomadic invaders eventually routed the Khitan, establishing the capital of the Jin Dynasty (1115–1234) on the outskirts of Beijing (which they renamed Zhongdu or Central Capital). The Jin capital was in turn completely razed by a fresh batch of northern nomadic usurpers. They were the Mongols – led by Genghis Khan – who would leave a more lasting and extensive mark on Beijing and all of China.

The Confucius Temple honours the influential philosopher

Genghis Khan laid the groundwork, gradually uniting all China under his rule and leaving it to his famous grandson, Kublai Khan, to secure the Yuan Dynasty (1279–1368). Kublai Khan founded his capital in 1279 on Beijing's Beihai Lake, where you can still see some of his imperial treasures. It was to these same shores that Marco Polo claimed to have journeyed at the end of the 13th century and won the support of Kublai Khan. He made Beijing, known as Khanbaliq (Khan's Town) or

Dadu (Great Capital), the base for his extensive travels in China as emissary of the Khan. Of the 13th-century capital, Marco Polo wrote that 'the whole interior of the city is laid out in squares like a chessboard with such masterly precision that no description can do justice to it' – a pattern Beijing retains to this day.

The Ming Period

The Mongol rulers of the Yuan Dynasty were eventually undone by indigenous Chinese rebels who established the long-running Ming Dynasty (1368–1644). The capital was again razed and rebuilt, and Emperor Yongle gave it a new name that would stick: Beijing (Northern Capital). By 1420 he had finished constructing the city's most famous surviving monument, the Forbidden City, along with the Bell Tower, the Drum Tower and the graceful Temple of Heaven. Many of Beijing's major temples also date from the Ming Dynasty.

The Ming Tombs are found to the northwest of Beijing

The Ming emperors cautiously welcomed a few Catholic missionaries from Europe to Beijing. In the 17th century the Jesuits, headed by Matteo Ricci, had a profound influence not so much on Chinese religion as on science, mathematics, astronomy, art, medicine and other forms of knowledge. Perhaps the greatest project of the Ming, however, was the restoration and extension of the Great Wall north of Beijing. For the first time, brick was used to finish these magnificent fortifications. It is the Ming Dynasty Great Wall that millions visit today at Beijing.

Ming emperor Wanli's crown

The Qing Period

The Ming rulers were understandably nervous about yet another invasion from the north, but despite the extension of the Great Wall, they were nonetheless undone by precisely what they feared most. This time the northern conquerors were the Manchus, who established a dynasty that proved as long-lived and as glorious as the Ming.

The Manchu rulers of the Qing Dynasty (1644–1911) were wise enough to adopt Chinese ways. They kept the capital at Beijing but, unlike preceding dynasties, did not raze it. Instead the Manchus preserved and restored China's past. The Forbidden City, the Temple of Heaven and Beihai Lake were kept as imperial strongholds. Old temples were restored and the *hutong* areas of courtyard mansions were developed.

Two of the greatest Qing emperors, Kangxi and his grandson Qianlong, maintained the Ming Tombs and built the original Summer Palace, while the last great imperial ruler, the Empress Dowager Cixi, built a new Summer Palace and kept the Forbidden City in splendid condition into the early 20th century. These and most other historic sites at Beijing were either preserved or created by the Qing rulers, including their own imperial tombs, which rival those of the Ming.

The Qing Dynasty is also celebrated for its elaboration of the artistic traditions it inherited from the Ming Dynasty. What we know as Beijing-style opera and still see performed today in the capital became formalised under the Qing, although its roots (and costumes) go back to Ming and earlier eras. The Ming were also noted for their superb ink paintings, cloisonné enamel work, furniture design and lacquerware – but above all for their porcelains of the 'five-colours' and 'blue-and-white' schools. At the end of the Ming, these porcelains with landscape and garden designs became all the rage in Europe, where imitation 'Chinese' pottery began to be produced. The Qing continued these artistic traditions, adding increasingly rich and dense ornamentation and applying new colours, many of them clashing or gaudy.

The Summer Palaces were constructed during Qing rule

In the 19th century the Qing rulers faced a new legion of invaders, not from the north (as in the past) but this time it was from the West, and they were unable to resist the tide.

Since the time of the First Opium War (1839–1842), Western nations had been pushing China to open its doors to foreign trade. In 1860, during the Second Opium War, British and French troops occupied Beijing and exacted treaty rights. Foreign delegations, businesses and missionaries poured into the capital and took up residence in the Legation Quarter, located just to the southeast of the Forbidden City.

In 1900, the Legation Quarter was attacked by the Boxers, a radical nationalist group that had the tacit support of the Qing court. In retaliation for this unsuccessful attempt to expel Westerners from Beijing, military

> ### Boxers defeated
>
> In the aftermath of the Boxer Rebellion, a foreign newspaper in Beijing reported: 'The capital of the emperors was partly destroyed, partly burned down. All that was left was a dead city. The streets were choked with the bodies of Chinese, many charred or eaten by stray dogs.'

forces representing the eight foreign nations resident in the capital went on the rampage, destroying the national library and even setting fire to the New Summer Palace *(see page 60)*. Thereafter, the Legation Quarter exercised complete control over its own affairs, becoming a foreign city within Beijing. Many of the European-style embassy buildings, offices, banks, hotels and mansions of the period have survived, although all have been converted to other uses. The American Legation is now an upmarket restaurant and bar complex.

Republicans and Warlords

China's history of imperial rule is far older than Beijing's reign as capital, but it was at Beijing that the last of China's dynasties was destined to fall. The Qing rulers were overthrown in 1911 and the Republic of China, led by Sun Yatsen, was declared.

A period of regional civil wars and power struggles among rival warlords ensued. Students used Tiananmen Square in 1919 as the stage for their protests against post-World War I 'unequal treaties' that favoured Japan in a demonstration known as the May the Fourth Movement. After this the

Revolutionary imagery

workers' movement began to grow and the Communist Party emerged. But in 1928, it was banned by the nationalist Guomindang Party, led by Chiang Kai-Shek, who moved the capital to Nanjing.

During this time, Beijing's citizens enjoyed greater freedom. For the first time in the city's history, the imperial strongholds, from the Forbidden City to the Temple of Heaven, were no longer forbidden to the Chinese masses. However, such progress proved short-lived. Japanese forces invaded northern China on the eve of World War II, seizing the city in 1937 after a valiant battle at the Marco Polo Bridge *(see page 67)*. The Japanese occupied Beijing until the war's end in 1945.

Communists and the Cultural Revolution

On 1 October 1949, a new nation – the People's Republic of China – was declared from the podium facing Tiananmen Square, and Beijing was again to serve as China's capital. This China was indeed radically new. Led by Chairman Mao Zedong, it was the largest communist state in the world and it would soon begin its own programme to reverse and destroy the 'feudal' legacy of thousands of years of imperial rule.

The Chinese Communist Party first initiated a popular programme of reconstruction to transform and modernise the nation. In Beijing, the ancient city walls were pulled down and the city moat was filled in. Only a few of the venerable city gates and towers remain today. China's first subway system now retraces the foundations of the city walls, with the stops named after the ancient city gates. Tiananmen Square was substantially enlarged, Chang'an Avenue widened, the Great Hall of the People built, the Museum of History and the Museum of the Revolution opened – all in the 1950s. Old neighbourhoods began to be replaced by modern brick-and-concrete high-rises. Beijing became its own powerful municipality (not part of any province), the seat of the nation's revolutionary government.

The Cultural Revolution (1966–76) closed Beijing's doors to the outside world. Mao and his most radical followers shut down the nation's institutions and went on a witch hunt for those alleged to harbour politically incorrect thoughts,

Maomorabilia

Away from Tiananmen Gate, the most likely place you will see the image of Mao Zedong is in one of the city's curio markets. The vast sea of kitsch created during the 1960s and early 1970s in his honour has, in recent years, become at least semi-fashionable.

Mao attained near Messianic status during the Cultural Revolution which began in 1966, a time when his likeness appeared on some two billion pictures and three billion badges. More than 350 million copies of the *Little Red Book* were printed between 1964 and 1966, and double-image Mao medallions, rubber stamps, resin busts and ceramic ornaments all fuelled the personality cult.

Despite the huge volume produced, some items have become valuable collectors' pieces. A few Cultural Revolution paintings have sold for more than $1 million. Many badges were thrown away or used as scrap, but Beijing's leading collector has reputedly salvaged over 100,000.

behaviours or backgrounds (i.e. anyone not waving Mao's *Little Red Book*). Many of Beijing's temples and historic sites were not only closed but badly damaged, all in order to make a complete break with the feudal, superstitious past. Renovations are still not complete and some ancient sites have never reopened.

A Modern Transformation

Nevertheless, after the death of Chairman Mao (whose mausoleum on Tiananmen Square has become a popular monument to China's modern 'emperor'), Beijing entered a period of liberal economic reform that has again transformed the capital. Under 'supreme leader' Deng Xiaoping, China opened up to Western investment and culture in the 1980s.

By the time of Deng's death in 1997, Beijing had firmly reshaped itself as an international capital in the Western mode, complete with expressways, skyscrapers, shopping plazas and state-of-the-art computer technologies – not to mention rising crime rates, increasing unemployment and income disparities sharp enough to make Mao turn over in his crypt.

The skyline of the capital keeps rising and preparations for the 2008 Olympics have dotted the city with grand sports venues. Today's Beijing may

On guard in Tiananmen Square

have little in common with the Beihai lakeshore of Kublai Khan and Marco Polo, the Forbidden City of the Ming, the Summer Palace of the Qing or even the patriotic tomb of Chairman Mao. But China's capital has not escaped the history that shaped it, be it ancient or modern. Visitors can still see both today.

Historical Landmarks

500,000BC Cave dwellers reside southwest of Beijing.

20,000BC Village established near Tiananmen Square site.

AD916–1125 Liao Dynasty establishes northern capital at Beijing.

1215 Genghis Khan's armies raze the city.

1275 Marco Polo visits Kublai Khan's capital, Khanbaliq (Beijing).

1406–20 Emperor Yongle rebuilds the city around the new Imperial Palace.

1644 Manchus claim Beijing as capital and begin the Qing Dynasty.

1840–2 First Opium War.

1858–60 Second Opium War. European forces invade Beijing and open Foreign Legation.

1900 The Boxer Rebellion.

1911 Qing Dynasty falls; Republic of China is declared.

1919 Protests in Tiananmen Square against foreign treaties.

1924 Pu Yi, China's last emperor, expelled from the Forbidden City.

1928 Chiang Kai-shek makes Nanjing China's capital.

1937 The Marco Polo Bridge incident.

1937–45 Beijing occupied by Japan.

1949 Beijing becomes the capital of the People's Republic of China under Mao Zedong.

1966 Cultural Revolution begins.

1972 US President Nixon visits Beijing and establishes diplomatic relations.

1976 Chairman Mao dies.

1989 Tiananmen Square massacre.

1997 Deng Xiaoping dies.

2003 Hu Jintao becomes president.

2005 China revalues the renminbi (yuan), moving to an exchange rate system that references a basket of currencies.

2006 Beijing–Lhasa train route is launched.

2007 China becomes the second-largest economy in the world after the US.

2008 Beijing hosts the Olympics amid protests from overseas about China's poor human rights and environmental record.

WHERE TO GO

Beijing has fascinating districts and neighbourhoods to explore. However, the main attractions are scattered throughout this sprawling city, so you'll be taking frequent taxi or subway rides no matter where your hotel is located. Following the ancient city plan, we have divided the capital like a compass, with the sights in the centre surrounded by quadrants to the north, south, east and west.

The main urban area of Beijing covers 750 sq km (290 sq miles), with the Forbidden City and Tiananmen Square at the heart. Chang'an Avenue (Xichang'an Jie/Dongchang'an Jie) bisects these two sites and forms the capital's long, wide east–west axis. A north–south axis runs 8km (5 miles) from the Temple of Heaven through the Forbidden City to the Drum and Bell towers. Old Beijing, once surrounded by city walls and nine towering gates, is now encircled by a modern subway and a major expressway, the Second Ring Road (23.5km/14½ miles).

In turn, a Third Ring Road, 48km (30 miles), encompasses most of urban Beijing, although the city is bulging outwards towards the Fourth, Fifth and Sixth ring roads.

The Forbidden City and Tiananmen Square in the city centre are convenient reference points for locating the attractions in the north, south, east and west districts of the city.

CITY CENTRE

The Forbidden City dominates the centre of Beijing and across Chang'an Avenue to the south is the capital's foremost modern site, Tiananmen Square. Just east of the Forbidden City is Beijing's most important shopping street,

Water calligraphy in Jingshan Park

Wangfujing Dajie. These three places are within walking distance of each other, a rarity for sightseeing in the capital.

Forbidden City

Completed by the Emperor Yongle in 1420, the **Forbidden City** (Zijin Cheng; 8am–4.30pm, until 5pm in summer; charge) was home to 24 consecutive rulers of China during the Ming (1368–1644) and Qing (1644–1911) dynasties. The 9-m (30-ft) walls enclose 74 hectares (183 acres) of magnificent halls, palaces, courtyards and imperial gardens, and the rooms and chambers number nearly 10,000. Today, the Forbidden City, also known as the Imperial Palace (Gugong), is a museum of imperial architecture, artefacts and private collections of the emperors. It is worth arriving early in the day and buying an all-inclusive ticket *(tao piao)* as some halls have exhibitions that otherwise require separate tickets.

Qing-style dress

The main entrance is from the south, through the **Tiananmen Gate** (Gate of Heavenly Peace), which is the large archway decorated with Chairman Mao's portrait facing Chang'an Avenue and Tiananmen Square. The ticket booth is due north along a central corridor at the **Meridian Gate** (Wumen). Here, audio guides can be hired in several different languages.

A dragon motif on an urn

Beyond the Meridian Gate is the Outer Courtyard, containing three magnificent ceremonial halls and their vast courtyards. The Meridian Gate is connected to the first great hall by the **Gate of Supreme Harmony** (Taihemen), which has five white marble bridges.

The first hall of the **Outer Courtyard**, known as the Hall of Supreme Harmony (Taihedian), contains the Dragon Throne, from where the emperors ruled. Only they could enter the hall by walking up the ramp adorned with dragon motifs. The courtyard's second hall, the Hall of Middle Harmony (Zhonghedian), contains a smaller throne, from which emperors addressed their ministers and prepared for ceremonies before entering the main hall. The third hall, called the Hall of Preserving Harmony (Baohedian), is where emperors received China's best students from the annual imperial examinations that determined who would enter the bureaucracy. All three halls, standing on a high marble platform, date from 1420 but were renovated or rebuilt under the Qing emperors.

Between the Inner and Outer courtyards are the **Eastern Exhibition Halls**. Here the Gate of Peace and Longevity (Ningshoumen) leads to the Palace of Peace and Longevity (Ningshougong), which Emperor Qianlong had built for his old age. The **Imperial Treasury** is housed in the adjoining halls to the north. The royal treasures include golden cutlery and table silver, jewellery, robes, porcelain and cloisonné.

Also located in this section of the Forbidden City are the Empress Dowager's private theatre, Emperor Qianlong's rock garden, the fascinating clock museum and the **Nine Dragon Screen** (Jiulongbi), a 30-m (96-ft) ceramic mosaic

The Palace Eunuchs

For nearly 2,000 years the emperors of China required that all male servants be eunuchs, thus protecting the honour of their wives and concubines. Working closely with rulers and members of the royal family, some of these castrated servants rose to positions of high power, amassing fortunes and sometimes directing affairs of state. Ming Dynasty rulers were said to have as many as 20,000 eunuchs in the Forbidden City but only 1,500 remained when the last dynasty fell in 1911.

Eunuchs came from the poorest ranks of the population, often snatched as children by buyers. Educated eunuchs might become secretaries or teachers in the Forbidden City, but most ended up working in the kitchen or gardens. They could be beaten for the slightest mistake by their masters – or even put to death.

Those few eunuchs who rose to positions of influence acquired enough wealth to buy houses, land and businesses outside the Forbidden City. Upon retirement, the wealthiest often moved to Buddhist monasteries where they had made large contributions. While castration was not always successful (and rumours of romances between eunuchs and palace maids were constant), the eunuchs were universally pitied, often reviled and despised and condemned to be outcasts.

created in 1773. The dragon is a symbol of heaven and, therefore, of the emperor, as is the number nine, the highest unit.

Three private pavilions make up the **Inner Courtyard,** located on the central axis in the northern portion of the Forbidden City. These halls were used as residences by the emperors and their families. The imperial concubines and eunuchs also lived here, with household staff often numbering over 1,000.

The imperial throne in the Palace of Heavenly Purity

The first pavilion is the Palace of Heavenly Purity (Qianqinggong), the private residence of the Ming emperors, later used by the Qing Dynasty for audiences with officials and foreign envoys. The inscription above the imperial throne reads 'just and honourable'. The second pavilion is the Hall of Union (Jiaotaian), which contains the throne of a Qing empress. The final hall is the Palace of Earthly Tranquillity (Kuninggong), where the last Chinese emperor, Pu Yi, was married as a child in 1922.

Near the northern gate to the Forbidden City is the **Imperial Flower Garden** (Yuhuayuan), filled with small pavilions, ancient cypress trees, flowers, bamboo and complex rockeries, all built during the Ming Dynasty. The final major pavilion is the Palace of Imperial Peace (Qin'an), a Daoist temple to Xuanwu, the God of Fire.

For a panoramic view of the entire Forbidden City, leave by way of the Gate of the Divine Warrior (Shenwumen) and cross the street to Jingshan Park *(see page 35)*.

Tiananmen Square

Occupying some 40 hectares (99 acres) directly south of the Forbidden City, **Tiananmen Square** (Tiananmen Guangchang) is the largest public square on earth. This vast expanse did not exist during the time of the emperors, but in the 20th century it became China's primary public meeting place for national ceremonies and political demonstrations. It was enlarged to its present size under Mao Zedong during the 1950s. In the late 1990s, to celebrate the 50th anniversary of the founding of the People's Republic on 1 October 1949, Tiananmen Square was renovated, with granite replacing the old paving blocks.

More than 500 years old, **Qianmen** (Front Gate), one of the original nine gates of the city wall, still stands at the southern end of Tiananmen Square. Most of the other gates fell when the wall was demolished during the modernisation programme carried out in Beijing in the late 1950s. The gate comprises two separate structures: the stone Jianlou (Arrow Tower), which burned down in the Boxer Rebellion of 1900 and was reconstructed in 1903; and the main gate, the wooden Zhengyangmen (Gate Facing the Sun), just to the north, also damaged in 1900 and reconstructed, to which the city wall was connected. The gates

Jianlou (Arrow Tower) forms the southern part of Qianmen

are free to walk through, and, for a modest fee, visitors can climb Zhengyangmen, at 40m (130ft), the tallest gate in Beijing (daily 8.30am–4pm). Zhengyangmen houses an interesting photographic exhibition of scenes from everyday life in old Beijing.

Also located on the south side of Tiananmen Square is the **Mao Zedong Mausoleum** (Mao Zhuxi Jiniantang; Tue–Sun 8am–noon; free), opened in 1977, a year after the Chairman's death. Especially popular with Chinese tourists, the mausoleum consists of a reception hall – with a statue of the Great Helmsman seated on his 'throne' – and an inner chamber, where Mao lies in state in a crystal

sarcophagus. Visitors maintain a respectful silence and are quickly ushered through to a gift shop at the back.

The **Monument to the People's Heroes** (Renmin Yinxiong Jinianbei), on the west side of the square, became internationally renowned when it served as the command post for pro-democracy demonstrators during the 1989 occupation of Tiananmen. The granite obelisk, 38m (124ft) high, was erected in 1958. It contains calligraphy carved in the hand of Chairman Mao and is engraved with stirring scenes of a century of Chinese revolutionary history.

The massive **Great Hall of the People** (Renmindahuitang; daily except when in session, 8.30am–3pm; charge) borders the west side of Tiananmen Square. It opened in 1958 and has served as China's legislative headquarters ever since. Whenever the National People's Congress is not in session, the Great Hall is open to visitors, who can peer

Standing to attention at the Monument to the People's Heroes

into its banquet halls, 32 reception rooms (one for each province and region) and glittering main auditorium, which holds up to 10,000 delegates.

Behind the Great Hall is the **China National Grand Theatre** (Zhongguo Guojia Dajuyuan), a striking-looking titanium and glass dome surrounded by water that opened in December 2007. The city's first unconventional modern building, the 'Eggshell', as it is known because of its shape, has an opera hall, a concert hall and a theatre.

Mao's portrait

As Mao's body lies in its mausoleum, his seemingly ageless likeness looks down from the Tiananmen Gate. The portrait of the leader measures 6m by 4½m (20ft by 15ft) and weighs nearly 1½ tons. It is cleaned every year before Labour Day (1 May) and replaced before National Day (1 October), when Mao is joined by Sun Yat-sen, founder of the Republic.

On the eastern side of Tiananmen Square, opposite the Great Hall of the People, is the **National Museum of China** (Zhongguo Guojia Bowuguan), which houses the Museum of the Chinese Revolution and the Museum of Chinese History. The museum is undergoing renovations and is not scheduled to reopen until 2010. Until then you can see many of its more than 6,000 pieces in the Capital Museum *(see page 57)*. Renovations have also temporarily closed the **Museum of the Chinese Revolution** (Zhongguo Geming Bowuguan). When it reopens it will chronicle the history of the Communist Party in China, the revolutionary civil wars and the campaign of resistance against the Japanese. The **Museum of Chinese History** (Zhongguo Lishi Bowuguan) provides an exhaustive overview of Chinese civilisation. Among the exhibits are ancient bronzes, jade pieces and bones, and ceramics from the Tang and Song dynasties. It, too, is affected by renovation work and at the moment has limited displays.

Inside the East Cathedral, where Mass is held on Sundays

Wangfujing Street

Beijing's top shopping street is also the site of many cultural and historic attractions. **Wangfujing Street** (Wangfujing Dajie) begins a few blocks east of the Forbidden City and runs north from Chang'an Avenue.

The **Beijing Hotel** (Beijing Fandian) began as the 'Grand Hotel de Pekin' under foreign management in 1917, has had several wings added and is now akin to an architectural museum of Beijing's evolution in the 20th century. Raffles Hotel Beijing, in all its colonial luxury chic, is now housed in the middle orange-brick section. Wangfujing itself has a long history, serving as the exclusive neighbourhood of the well-connected and the rich during the Ming and Qing dynasties. Westerners moved to the district in the late-19th century and the street was known as Morrison Street for a time, after a *Times* correspondent. Tradesmen had long done business in the neighbourhood's tiny lanes, which are today filled with an assortment of tea shops, silk stores, art galleries, street markets and modern shopping plazas.

The southern end is dominated by the **Oriental Plaza**, a sprawling two-floor complex featuring designer outlets and a food court. This modern retail complex is in fact situated on the capital's oldest site – a 20,000-year-old Stone Age settlement. The excavation unearthed human fossils, buffalo bones and hunting tools.

Sun Dong An Plaza (at No. 38 Wangfujing) has seven levels of boutiques, supermarkets and fast-food outlets.

Opposite is the **Foreign Language Bookstore** (at No. 235), holding the capital's largest collection of non-Chinese books and magazines. Walk one block north to find **St Joseph's Catholic Church** (Dongtang), the 'East Cathedral' that was levelled during the Boxer Rebellion (1900) and immediately rebuilt; it is now open for Sunday Mass.

At the far northern end of the street is the **China National Art Gallery** (Mei Shu Guan; daily 9am–5pm; charge). Within this monumental museum, built in 1959, are 14 galleries with contemporary as well as traditional artworks.

NORTH BEIJING

The neighbourhoods north of the Forbidden City are the most scenic in Beijing, encompassing imperial parks and lakes, temples and towers, princely mansions and some of the city's most interesting older neighbourhoods. An atmosphere of imperial leisure is cast by **Jingshan Park** (Jingshan Gongyuan), also called Coal Hill (Meishan), rising immediately north of the Forbidden City. Jingshan was built by hand from soil dug out of the palace moat in the early 15th century. A 10-minute hike to the summit at the **Pavilion of Everlasting Spring** (Wanchungting) is

View across the Forbidden City from the top of Jingshan Park

rewarded by the finest view possible of the Forbidden City and its golden-tiled palaces. To the right (west) of the old Forbidden City is a new version, Zhongnanhai, where China's communist leaders are ensconced today (strictly off-limits to all visitors).

Beihai Park

Beijing's oldest imperial garden, **Beihai Park** (Beihai Gongyuan; park: daily 7am–8pm, until 9pm in winter; buildings: daily 8am–5pm; charge – an all-inclusive ticket *(tao piao)* allows access to all places of interest within the park), was built on the capital's largest lake over 800 years ago. Near the south entrance, in the Round City (Tuancheng), is a large ceremonial vessel of green jade presented in 1265 to Kublai Khan, who built a palace here and entertained Marco Polo on these lake shores in the 13th century.

Beihai's White Dagoba

Scenic Hortensia Island (Qionghuadao), built from the soil excavated to create Beihai's lake, is crowned by the **White Dagoba** (Baita), one of Beijing's landmarks. Tibetan in style, this *dagoba* commemorates a visit by the Dalai Lama in 1651 and is 36m (118ft) high. At its foot on Jade Hill, to the south, is the Temple of Eternal Peace (Yong'ansi), a well-preserved Lamaist Buddhist complex.

The north shore of the island is bordered by a covered walkway, known as the Painted Gallery, and a cluster of Qing Dynasty imperial halls. Located here is a traditional restaurant, Fangshan, founded by chefs who cooked for the last emperor in the Forbidden City.

On the western shore of Beihai's lake are several pavilions and gardens built during the Qing Dynasty,

Beihai Park is a popular location for weddings

including a fine rock and water garden, Haopujian, where the Empress Dowager Cixi listened to music. The Studio of the Painted Boat (Huafangzhai) is another shore garden, built by Emperor Qianlong in the 18th century, famous for its large square stone pool. On the northern shore of the lake is the Place of the Quiet Heart (Jingxinzhai), a favourite retreat of China's last emperor, Pu Yi. On the eastern shore is a double-sided Nine Dragon Screen (Jiulongbi), created in the 18th century from glazed tiles, similar to the one in the Forbidden City.

The pavilions, pagodas and rockeries on the northeast shore are known collectively as the Gardens Within Gardens, where the imperial court once enjoyed the lake. Its most arresting site is **Miniature Western Heaven** (Xiaoxitian), which consists of a square pagoda and four towers, erected as a shrine to the Goddess of Mercy (Guanyin) in 1770. Tour boats depart the eastern shore from Five Dragons Pavilion to Hortensia Island. Today, Beihai lake is no longer restricted to the imperial court and it is the most popular spot in Beijing to rent a rowing boat in the summer or to ice skate in the winter.

Yinding Bridge, where two back lakes meet *(see page 40)*

Back Lakes District

Central Beijing's three front lakes, Nanhai, Zhongnanhai and Beihai, run along the west side of the Forbidden City from Chang'an Avenue north to where they connect with the three **Back Lakes**, known as Qianhai, Houhai and Xihai. These lakes once comprised the route used to ship grain and luxuries via the Grand Canal to the Forbidden City. Later, this was the waterway employed by imperial barges when the emperor desired an outing. These interconnected lakes are marvellous places to stroll. The Back Lakes District contains many landmarks of old Beijing – from mansions to old temples and gardens – but it is best known for its colourful alleyways and traditional courtyard houses. In recent years, numerous restaurants, bars and cafés have been established along the lake shore, making the area a major focus of the capital's nightlife.

At the northern tip of the Back Lakes is **Huifeng Temple** (Huifengsi). Perched on a tiny rocky isle in Xihai Lake, it is a wonderful spot for a lake view and a picnic. To the east of this temple, on the north side of the Second Ring Road, is Deshengmen Arrow Tower, a gate and archers' tower dating from the Ming Dynasty that survived the demolition of the great city wall.

On the eastern shore of Houhai Lake, the middle of the three Back Lakes, is the **Song Qingling Residence** (Song Qingling Guzhu), where the famous Song sister who married Sun Yat-sen lived from 1963 until her death in 1981. Her estate and its 200-year-old classical garden are now a museum, filled with photographs and heirlooms of her remarkable life. On the same lake shore is **Guanghua Temple** (Guanghua Si), a small Buddhist complex that has

Hutong

The neighbourhoods of the Back Lakes District are filled with the *hutong* (alleys) and *siheyuan* (courtyard houses) that were characteristic of urban Beijing during the Ming and Qing dynasties. They are common even today, with nearly half of the capital's population living in some form of rectangular courtyard compound. Nevertheless, *hutong* and *siheyuan* are endangered symbols of Beijing's past, constantly under threat of urban renewal. Fewer than 2,000 courtyard dwellings are preserved in cultural protection zones. Although it would have once been occupied by a single rich family (plus servants), a courtyard house today is shared by many families.

You can explore the *hutong* on your own – on foot, by rented bicycle, or by hiring one of the canopied pedicabs in the area, but most visitors prefer a guided tour. The Beijing Hutong Tourist Agency (tel: 6615-9097), which books tours through hotel desks, has a fleet of red-canopied pedicabs led by an English-speaking guide. Its *hutong* tour combines many of the sights in the Back Lakes District with the opportunity to step inside a courtyard house and talk with its modern-day residents.

Inside the Drum Tower

returned to life after being severely damaged by rampaging Red Guards during the Cultural Revolution (1966–1976). Nearly two dozen monks reside here.

A few blocks east of the Guanghua Temple are Beijing's historic **Drum Tower** (Gulou) and **Bell Tower** (Zhonglou). Both can be climbed for splendid views of the Back Lakes District. The Drum Tower (daily 9am–5pm; charge) is the more interesting of the two. The capital's first Drum Tower, from which the hours of the day were signalled with drums, was built here by Kublai Khan in 1272, rebuilt by Ming Emperor Yongle in 1420 and renovated under the Qing emperors. A side stairway leads to the balcony, where one of the 24 original watch drums remains, along with what's claimed to be the world's largest drum (made in 1990).

Qianhai, the most southern of the Back Lakes, connects to the lake in Beihai Park. Upmarket bars and restaurants line Qianhai Lake's southwestern shore, along Lotus Lane. Another nightlife area is concentrated around **Yinding Bridge** (Silver Ingot Bridge), where Houhai joins Qianhai Lake.

On the west side of the Back Lakes is the **Palace of Prince Gong** (Gong Wang Fu; daily 8.30am–4.30pm; charge), Beijing's best-preserved example of an imperial mansion. Prince Gong, brother to an emperor and father of China's last emperor, Pu Yi, occupied this estate in the mid-19th century, making use of its 31 halls and pavilions as his private residence. The estate contains numerous courtyards, arched bridges, ponds, rock gardens and its own pagoda.

Lama Temple

Beijing's most popular Buddhist complex is the **Lama Temple** (Yonghegong; daily 9am–4.30pm; charge) in the northeast of the city on the Second Ring Road. Built in 1694 for a prince who became the Qing Emperor Yongzheng, it was converted to a temple in 1744. Under the reign of Qianlong the temple served as the chief centre of Tibetan Buddhism (Yellow Hat sect) outside of Lhasa. The Lama Temple is large and ornate, with about 200 monks in residence today.

Its five central worship halls are spacious. Between the first and second halls is the capital's oldest incense burner (1747). The throne of the Dalai Lama is in the fourth worship hall (Falundian). The final hall contains the Lama Temple's most revered statue, a 23-m (75-ft) image of the Buddha carved from a Tibetan sandalwood tree, its head peeking out of the pavilion's third storey. The side halls have large collections

The Lama Temple is one of the city's most beautiful temples

of cast and carved Buddhist figures, including many Tantric statues whose more explicit features are discreetly draped in colourful silk scarves.

Confucius Temple

A short distance west of the usually packed Lama Temple is the serene **Confucius Temple** (Kong Miao; daily 8.30am–5pm; charge), the largest shrine to the great philosopher outside of Confucius' hometown, Qufu. Built in 1302, the complex was long part of the Imperial College (Guozijian) and its courtyards teem with scores of carved stone tablets honouring students who passed the nationwide civil service examinations from the time of Kublai Khan. Both the temple and the academy next door (see below) have been refurbished and are now combined under one entrance ticket.

In the front courtyard of the temple are almost 200 stone tablets (steles) recording the names of those scholars who passed the imperial exams. At the north end of the complex there is a statue of Confucius and a collection of 18th-century stone drums used in Confucian ceremonies. **The Imperial Academy** started as a school to teach Mongolian and Chinese. Its old lecture halls and tree-filled courtyards have a learned atmosphere.

SOUTH BEIJING

Beyond the Temple of Heaven and Liulichang Culture Street, the Xuanwu and Chongwen districts south of Tiananmen Square are comparatively less explored by tourists. But there are a number of sights of interest here and the area itself holds a certain charm, having changed less than any other part of the city over the past 25 years. The buildings are lower, the pavements narrower, and the life on the streets more frenetic. But the housing here is often sub-standard and the distinctive character of the neighbourhood will inevitably change for the benefit of the inhabitants, as the Beijing Government carries out much-needed regeneration.

Foreign Legation

The **Foreign Legation**, where foreign governments maintained their own autonomous quarter in Beijing from 1860 to 1937, lies east of Tiananmen Square. No longer the site of the capital's diplomatic compounds, this district still contains many former embassies, clubs, barracks, churches and commercial buildings, most now Chinese government buildings, banks and offices. The architecture is fascinating. Located along Taijichang Dajie (the former Customs Street), directly south of Dongchang'an Jie (Chang'an Avenue East), are the old Austro-Hungarian Legation (now the Institute of International Studies), the Italian Legation (now the Chinese People's

Beijing's Hui Muslim population is concentrated in the south

Association for Friendship with Foreign Countries), the private Peking Club (now the Beijing People's Congress) and the French Legation (now the offices of the Chinese Workers Union).

West along Jiaominxiang towards Tiananmen Square is St Michael's Church, built in 1902 by the French. You'll also find the German Hospital (now the Beijing Hospital) here and the former embassies of Germany, France, Spain, Holland and Russia.

Many Beijingers still rely on pedal power to get around

North up Zhengyi Lu (the former Canal Street) back towards Chang'an Avenue are the former Japanese Legation (the Beijing mayor's office) and the British Legation, once the largest Western stronghold in Beijing, now the stronghold of the Chinese security services.

Catholics, Muslims and Buddhists

Southwest of Tiananmen Square, in the city's Xuanwu District, is the city's main Catholic church, **South Cathedral** (Nantang). It was constructed on the site of missionary Matteo Ricci's residence in 1650 and rebuilt in 1904 after being destroyed during the Boxer Rebellion. Offering Masses in Chinese, Latin and English, South Cathedral has a rock garden dedicated to the Virgin.

Southwest Beijing is also the location of the **Ox Street Mosque** (Niu Jie Qingzhensi; daily 9am–5pm; charge), the centre of Beijing's most vibrant Muslim quarter. Here the capital's 200,000 Hui minority – largely indistinguishable from Beijing's Han Chinese majority – practise Islam, which arrived in China via the Silk Road during the Tang Dynasty (618–907). This mosque, originally constructed in the year 996, is Chinese in style but contains a six-sided astronomical tower, an Islamic prayer hall facing Mecca and tombs of Muslim leaders dating to the time of Kublai Khan.

The **Temple of the Source of Buddhist Teaching** (Fayuansi; Thur–Tue 8.30am–4pm; charge), near the Ox Street Mosque, dates from the Tang Dynasty (696) and houses a national Buddhist college and religious publishing house. In addition to dozens of novice monks in training, this large temple is famous for its Ming- and Qing-era statues, carved stone tablets, bells and incense burners.

Bicycling Beijing

Beijing still has its wide cycle lanes, and many people still choose to travel by bicycle despite the fact that about 1,000 new cars are added to the capital's roads every day. Visitors can hire bicycles – including multispeed mountain bikes – by the hour or day from many hotels and rental outlets. There's a bike repairman on nearly every corner to mend flat tyres cheaply on the spot.

With the recent increase in the number of private cars, cycling in Beijing is not as pleasurable – or as safe – as it once was. However, it is still a good way to see the city, especially in quieter areas such as Sanlitun. Beijing's major streets have spacious separate bicycle lanes which cars, trucks and buses are not supposed to use (but sometimes do). Otherwise, cars and pedestrians do have the right of way. Use your bell at crossroads to warn pedestrians.

Despite the large number of bicycles on the roads, they are on the decline. They have also been banned from one of its busiest streets (Xisi Dong Lu, near the Xidan shopping district). Apparently, the 100 bikes a minute there obstructed the timely flow of motorised vehicles.

Grand View Garden (Daguanyuan), situated at the southwest corner of the Second Ring Road, was opened in 1986 on the site of the imperial vegetable gardens. Built to recreate the garden portrayed in the popular Chinese novel *The Dream of the Red Chamber*, it contains lakes, pavilions, arched bridges and pagodas typical of Mandarin estates of the 18th century.

Temple of Heaven

The **Temple of Heaven** (Tiantan), constructed under Ming Emperor Yongle in 1420 as a site for sacred rites, is situated directly south of the Forbidden City. Today the site is called the **Temple of Heaven Park** (Tiantan Gongyuan; park: daily 6am–8pm; temple complex 8am–5.30pm; charge). It is easy to get here from the city centre by subway or by taxi, and the park can be entered through several gates.

The Temple of Heaven's Hall of Prayer for Good Harvests

Every year at the time of the winter solstice the emperor would lead a procession from the palace to the altar here to perform the annual rites and sacrifices to heaven, honouring his ancestors and praying for a good harvest in the season to come. The observation of such ritual was more than a mere formality. As the Son of Heaven, the emperor was believed to administer heavenly authority on Earth. According to the Chinese, natural catastro-

Music in Tiantan Park

phes, failing harvests and increasing corruption signalled that the emperor was out of favour with Heaven and his ancestors. In such circumstances, it was considered a legitimate act to overthrow him. Therefore, exact attention to the practice of the sacrificial rites in the Temple of Heaven was given the appropriate importance by the ever-wary emperor.

One of China's most remarkable architectural works survives from that era, the **Hall of Prayer for Good Harvests** (Qiniandian), a circular hall with blue-tiled roofs capped by a golden sphere. The entire shrine was built without nails or cross beams, its magnificent arched ceiling supported by 28 carved pillars. This hall survived until 1889, when lightning burned it to the ground, but the reconstruction is superb, and the round hall has become an emblem of imperial Beijing. Unfortunately, its ornate interior can only be glimpsed from outside, since visitors are no longer allowed within.

Two other important monuments survive in Tiantan Park, both located on the axis running south from the Hall of

Prayer for Good Harvests. The **Imperial Vault of Heaven** (Huangqiongyu), built in 1530, resembles the Hall of Prayer; stone tablets used in the winter solstice rituals were once stored here. It is surrounded by Echo Wall, into which visitors attempt to whisper messages that can be heard by friends at distant points along the wall. The **Altar of Heaven** (Yuanqiu), dating from 1530, is where silk was once burned as a sacrifice to the heavenly powers. Its acoustics are said to allow orations to be broadcast for miles in all directions.

Temple of Heaven Park is a nice place for a stroll. It's popular with locals, including citizens doing their *tai chi* exercises, musicians playing traditional Chinese instruments and men playing dominoes or Go.

Hunt for bargains and antique goods at the Panjiayuan Market

Outside the Park

By the west gate of the Temple of Heaven, the **Natural History Museum** (Ziran Bowuguan; Tue–Sun 8.30am–4pm; charge) has China's best display of dinosaur skeletons, from a giant one-horned Qingdaosaurus to a parrot-beaked specimen no bigger than a cat. The museum features exhibits in the fields of palaeontology, zoology and botany, but captions are in Chinese only.

Just across the street from the Temple of Heaven's east gate, across a footbridge, is the **Hongqiao Market** (Pearl

Market; daily 8.30am–7pm). Four floors of this twin-towered building are given over to densely packed stalls selling clothing, shoes, fake designer goods, antiques, silk and, especially, pearls. China now supplies 95 percent of the world market of cultured freshwater pearls. Quality has steadily improved. Most pearl vendors come from families that produce cultured freshwater pearls, and will string pearls to order. Be sure to bargain, ask that knots be tied between each pearl and buy a good clasp.

Chinese lanterns for sale

About 4km (2½ miles) to the east, past Longtan Park, is the **Panjiayuan Market** (Ghost Market; Huawei Lu Dajie). Also known as the Dirt Market, it offers a vast array of goods, from scroll paintings and porcelain to silk and Mao memorabilia, and is best visited as early as possible on Sunday morning.

By the ring road to the south is **Beijing Curio City** (Dongsanhuan Nan Lu, west of Huawei Bridge), four floors filled with more antiques, paintings, jewellery and furniture. It also has a duty-free shop, but remember to bring your passport, or you will not be allowed to buy anything.

Qianmen District

Just to the south of Tiananmen Square, beyond the Qianmen Gate, is the area referred to as Qianmen. In contrast to the tranquil temples and spacious imperial estates to the north, this area was once a bustling mass of everyday life and earthly pursuits, home to opera theatres as well as brothels and opium dens, so renowned that Manchu officials and even emperors in disguise would come to sample their pleasures. Qianmen was also known for its shops and restaurants and many survive.

Qianmen Street (Qianmen Dajie) has been rebuilt to appear as it would in the bustling 1920s, with old-style shops. There is a tramway, but no cars are allowed. The flavour of the old capital's commercial districts is perhaps best preserved along Liulichang and Dazhalan, two conjoined avenues that run east–west for over 1½km (1 mile). **Liulichang Culture Street** (Liulichang Xijie and Liulichang Dongjie), the shopping haunt of scholars and antiques fanciers since the Ming Dynasty, was restored in the 1980s. Its tile-roofed shops selling curios, antiques, scrolls and paintings include Rongbaozhai (art and art supplies), the China Bookstore (old books), Jiguge (a teahouse) and Wenshenzhai (former purveyor of lanterns to the Qing Dynasty).

Liulichang merges with **Dazhalan**, a cobblestone street closed to motor traffic that offers still more shopping: outlets for traditional herbal medicines, shoes, pickles, and silk fabric and clothing. The eastern end is intersected by Zhubaoshi Jie (Jewellery Street), once the major theatre and brothel district of Beijing and now a lively bazaar.

Among the small shops and restaurants to the east of Qianmen Dajie and south of Qianmen Dongdajie is Beijing's **Underground City** (Dixia Cheng; daily 8.30am–5pm; charge), a network of tunnels and bunkers built amid fears of Soviet attack following the 1960 bust-up between the countries. The vast tunnel system was never needed, but has since been used for everything from growing mushrooms to training athletes.

Going underground

To reach the entrance of the Underground City at 62 Xidamochang Jie, turn south from Qianmen Dongdajie into Zhengyi Lu, then left at the end, first right and then left again at the T-junction.

The National Aquatics Centre is known as the 'Water Cube'

EAST BEIJING

The areas east of Tiananmen Square along Chang'an Avenue and northeast up the Third Ring Road (both sections of the Chaoyang District) have received the lion's share of Beijing's modernisation. Here Chang'an Avenue changes its name to Jianguomenwai Dajie, the location of fine international hotels and excellent shopping, and it's a similar scene around the northeast section of the Third Ring Road. Between these two stretches is the Sanlitun Diplomatic Compound, with some of the capital's liveliest nightlife. Chaoyang is also home to most of the dazzling sports venues built for the 2008 Olympics.

Jianguomen

The eastern section of Chang'an Avenue, between the Second and Third ring roads, is known as **Jianguomen** (after one of old Beijing's nine city gates, now the site of a subway

Friendship Store

From dried mushrooms to exquisite cloisonné, you can buy almost anything produced in China at the Friendship Store (Youyi Shangdian) on Jianguomenwai Dajie. There's a large carpet section and a stock of good silk. It also has a dressmaking department, watch repair counter, bookshop, supermarket, dry cleaner's and tea shop. The Friendship Store can arrange to send any goods abroad and will also deal with the customs formalities for you.

station). A number of international hotels and shops can be found here.

At the intersection of Jianguomenwai Dajie and the Third Ring Road East there is a major shopping mall in the massive **China World Trade Centre**. This area is known as the central business district and is the site of some amazing skyscrapers. China World Trade Centre III will be the capital's tallest building at 330m (1,100ft). Opposite is the Yintai Centre, home of the luxurious Park Hyatt. Most remarkable of all is the twisted Z of the China Central Television Tower on Guanghua Lu and on the other side of the Third Ring Road. Other shopping options along Jianguomenwai Dajie include the Friendship Store, the best place to browse for Chinese gifts and souvenirs, and the Silk Street Market, in a multi-storey building, which sells silks, souvenirs and clothing.

Just north of the Friendship Store is **Ritan Park** (Ritan Gongyuan), where the Altar of the Sun stood in imperial days. The altar – where the emperor performed annual rites – was erected on a hill in 1530 which is today crowned by a pavilion.

Ancient Observatory

Beijing's **Ancient Observatory** (Gu Guanxiangtai; Tue–Sun 9am–4pm; charge) was built in 1442 under the Ming Dynasty. It is at the intersection of Jianguomenai Dajie and the Second Ring Road East; almost immediately below it is a subway station. The observatory supplanted one created by Kublai Khan. Inside the brick tower, which looks like a remnant of the old city wall, are astronomical displays, including a gold foil map of the heavens as they were plotted in China 500 years ago. On the open roof is a fine collection of Qing Dynasty bronze instruments (copies) devised by the Jesuit missionaries who resided in Beijing in the 17th century. The view from the terrace of the Forbidden City and Tiananmen Square is superb.

Sanlitun

In the heart of a large foreign diplomatic district between Dongzhimenwai Dajie and the Liangma River, **Sanlitun** is a major nightlife district. Many of its bars and cafés – offering international cuisine by day and drinking and music by night – are located on Sanlitun Lu, which has been officially named Sanlitun Bar Street (Sanlitun Jiuba Jie). Many of Beijing's expatriates and foreign tourists, as well as the city's younger locals, gather here in summer to sit at outside tables drinking, dining and people-watching. The area is currently undergoing large-scale reconstruction, and the range of malls and 'entertainment complexes' being erected promise to change the atmosphere. Another hotspot for clubbing and drinking is the Workers'

Sanlitun is a nightlife hotspot

Stadium, a five-minute walk west of Sanlitun. While Sanlitun is devoid of historic sites, it stands out as modern Beijing's most international neighbourhood. Another nightlife area has developed further east, around Chaoyang Park.

WEST BEIJING

The western precincts of Beijing are the site of some of its top attractions. Closest to the city centre are four major temples, two fascinating museums and the Beijing Zoo. The sumptuous Summer Palace and the evocative Western Hills are further out, northwest of the capital's urban sprawl. This is the beautiful, hilly countryside of the Haidian District (home to China's top universities and computer technology developers).

White Cloud Temple

White Cloud Temple

Beijing's most active Daoist complex, Baiyunguan, is better known as **White Cloud Temple** (daily 8.30am–4pm; charge). This is also the capital's most fascinating religious site, a place of superstition and incense, mystery and spirited worship. As China's leading indigenous religion, Daoism differs from Buddhism (transplanted from India) not so much in the architecture of its temples and the art of its statuary (these are often quite similar in style) as in its practices and beliefs. In its abstract form Daoism emphasises nature, the individual and the Way; in its organised form it relies on a huge pantheon of gods, goddesses and supernatural icons promising miracles.

At Baiyunguan the first courtyard features the Wind Containing Bridge, where visitors attempt to ensure their good fortune by strik-

A Daoist monk

ing a 17th-century copper bell with coins. In the Spring Hall for the Jade Emperor, worshippers touch the golden feet of statues representing the gods of wealth. In the side halls there are shrines where the devout can appeal to the proper god to cure eye problems, ensure the birth of a son, pass an examination, get a good job and increase longevity. Every one of these 'wishing halls' is usually jammed with locals, who are often dressed in their most expensive clothes for the tour. Festivals on the first and fifteenth of the lunar month are especially lively times to visit. At the rear of the complex there is a large rock garden, a courtyard and classrooms where many novice monks are trained in Daoism.

Baiyunguan was founded in 739 and received its present name in 1394. Most of the halls date from the Qing Dynasty, although Yuanchen Hall, where visitors try to locate the deity on the zodiac of their birthday, dates from the time of Kublai Khan. Just south of this temple complex is **Tianning Si**, the Temple of Heavenly Tranquillity, built during the Liao Dynasty (907–1125), making it Beijing's oldest surviving building. The 13-storey pagoda is 58m (190ft) high and is decorated with fine Buddhist carvings.

White Pagoda Temple

Extensively renovated and enlarged in 1998, the **White Pagoda Temple** (Baitasi; daily 8.30am–4.30pm; charge) is renowned for its Tibetan-style pagoda (usually called a *dagoba* or *stupa*). The white pagoda at this temple is the largest of its type in China, built in 1279 during the reign of Kublai Khan.

The main gate of the White Pagoda Temple (on the north side of Fuchengmennei Dajie), the first courtyard and the museum are new. The museum houses many Buddhist artefacts and statues discovered in the temple grounds, as well as a *sutra* copied out by Emperor Qianlong. This rare manuscript, unearthed in 1978, was composed in the Emperor's own hand in 1753. Beyond the museum to the north are three finely restored prayer halls. The Hall of the Great Enlightened Ones is stuffed with thousands of little Buddhas. The white pagoda itself, rising 51m (167ft), is last and, like most *dagobas,* remains sealed, its holy treasures and relics somewhere beneath or inside the imposing structure.

Five Pagoda Temple

North of Beijing Zoo, across the Nanchang River, is the beautiful **Five Pagoda Temple** (Wutasi; daily 8am–4pm; charge). Built in 1473 during the early Ming Dynasty, its main hall consists of a square stone building 7½m (25ft) high, its outside walls decorated with 1,000 niches, each containing an engraved Buddha. The hall is crowned with a cluster of five elaborate towering pagodas, more Indian than Chinese in style, with stairs inside leading up to a view from the roof.

The temple was originally part of the larger Zhengjue Temple complex (built during the reign of Ming Emperor Yongle in the 1420s and sacked by Western troops in 1860 and 1900). On the same grounds today is the **Beijing Stone Engraving Art Museum**, an open-air display of over 500 ancient stone carvings and inscribed stone pillars.

The Temple of Longevity, home of the Beijing Art Museum

Two Museums

Doubling as museum and temple, the **Beijing Art Museum** (Beijing Yishu Bowuguan; daily 9am–4.30pm; charge), to the west of the zoo and Purple Bamboo Park, is housed in the halls of **Wanshousi**, the Temple of Longevity. Although the temple, renovated in 1761 by Emperor Qianlong, is no longer active, it contains many old structures, including the bell and drum towers in the first courtyard, which date from 1577. The museum's wide-ranging collection includes Zhou Dynasty bronzes, and Ming and Qing paintings. At the rear of the temple is a large rock garden with shrines to the gods of three of Buddhism's sacred mountains in China, two pavilions built in 1761 and two 18th-century European-style arched gates.

While the National Museum is being overhauled, the **Capital Museum** (Tue–Sun 9am–5pm; charge) is the city's main show house for historical artefacts. The museum, set out like a giant shopping mall, is just west of White Cloud Temple

Giant panda in Beijing Zoo

next to Muxidi subway station. Escalators in genteel rows transport visitors to the six floors of exhibition rooms, which boast digital displays, recreations of old streets and shops and an ox-red marital bed. Look out for the travelling exhibitions.

Beijing Zoo

Beijing Zoo (Beijing Dongwuyuan; daily 7.30am–4.30pm; charge) is the creation of Empress Dowager Cixi, who in 1908 converted this private Ming Dynasty garden estate into a preserve for some 700 exotic animals imported from Germany. The entrance gate dates from the late Qing Dynasty and many of the exhibition halls seem nearly as old. With some 6,000 animals the zoo is the largest in China, but despite its notable collection of giant pandas, Siberian tigers, golden monkeys and red-crowned cranes, the facility is in need of modernisation. Few foreign visitors are happy with the size and condition of the cages, although the Panda Garden is a bit more spacious. The adjacent Beijing Aquarium, a state-of-the-art marine park, has over 50,000 aquatic species in residence.

Big Bell Temple

Directly north of the zoo on the Third Ring Road stands the **Big Bell Temple** (Dazhongsi; daily 8.30am–4.30pm; charge), aptly named in 1743, when the largest bronze bell in China was placed here. This huge bell, weighing 34,000kg (46 tons) and measuring 7m (23ft) high, was cast in 1420, just as the Forbidden City was completed. It is on display in its own pavilion at the rear of the temple. Locals often climb the stairs to the top and drop coins through an opening for good luck, a long-standing tradition with pilgrims to the temple.

Since the early 1980s the Big Bell Temple has served as China's bell museum, with over 700 bells in its collection. A few of the bells are modern (cast to commemorate recent events) and some are from foreign countries, but most are Chinese antiques. Among the bells displayed in the various halls and pavilions are some that are 4,000 years old. For a small charge, visitors can sound a set of stone chimes that date from the Warring States Period (475–221BC).

China's Harvard

China's top institution of higher learning, not far from the Summer Palace, is Peking University (also called Beijing University or 'Beida'). For over a century it has been the prime school for Chinese intellectuals and political theorists, as well as the source of student protest movements that have changed the course of the nation. Founded in 1898 as the Imperial University, it was renamed Peking University in 1911 with the fall of the Qing Dynasty. Mao Zedong worked here as a library assistant in 1918. In 1953, it was moved to its present campus and a new US$1.2 million library is the first of several dozen building projects that are giving the venerable campus a modern makeover.

Peking University's students first took their progressive agenda to Tiananmen Square in 1919, denouncing World War I treaties imposed by the West and decrying China's weakness and corruption. They appeared at Tiananmen again in 1976 to denounce the policies of Chairman Mao. Then, in 1989, they spearheaded the occupation of Tiananmen Square, calling for greater economic and political freedoms.

Peking University today is no hotbed of political dissent; students of 'China's Harvard' now seem more intent on pursuing business careers.

The Summer Palaces

Pailou gateway at the entrance to the New Summer Palace

There are two 'summer palaces' in the northwestern suburbs of Beijing. Between them, they were used by the Qing emperors for more than 150 years. During this time dozens of palaces, pavilions and temples were built in contrived idyllic landscapes of artificial hills, lakes and canals. The older complex, Yuanmingyuan, was largely destroyed by foreign soldiers in 1860 at the end of the Second Opium War.

The 'New' Summer Palace, Yiheyuan, built as a replacement by the Empress Dowager Cixi at the end of the 19th century, was also plundered by foreign troops, during the Boxer Rebellion of 1900. This time, however, most of the buildings survived or were restored. Like the Forbidden City, the Summer Palace was opened to the public in 1925, and today it is one of Beijing's major sights, attracting large numbers of visitors, particularly on summer weekends.

The 280-hectare (700-acre) **New Summer Palace** (Yiheyuan; daily summer 7am–6pm, winter 7am–5pm; charge) is dominated by **Kunming Lake**, which itself is subdivided into West Lake and South Lake by several causeways. **Longevity Hill** rises above the north shore. Behind its peaks is a version of Beijing's Back Lakes, created during the Qing Dynasty. The main strolling area is along the north shore of Kunming Lake, where the pavilions and courtyards are linked by the **Long Corridor** (Chang Lang).

This covered promenade stretches 777m (2,550ft) from the Eastern Halls west to the Marble Boat. First built in 1750, it consists of 273 crossbeam sections and four pavilions. Nearly every exposed portion of its beams, panels and pillars is decorated with a painted scene from Chinese myth, history or literature.

Among the important imperial buildings on the east side of the Long Corridor, four are worth viewing. The Hall of Benevolent Longevity (Renshou Dian) is where Empress Dowager Cixi received court members from her Dragon Throne (which is still in place). The Hall of Jade Ripples (Yulan Dian) is where Cixi confined her nephew, Emperor Guangxu, while she ruled in his place. The Hall for Cultivating Happiness (Yile Dian) served as the Empress Dowager's private viewing box for performances in the adjacent three-storey theatre, which was built to honour her 60th birthday. Cixi celebrated many of her birthdays at the Summer Palace and she was especially fond of theatrical performances, in which she sometimes played a role. This theatre now contains some of her imperial garments, jewellery and cosmetics, as well as a Mercedes Benz said to be the first passenger car in China. The Long Corridor begins at a fourth Qing building, the

Overlooking Kunming Lake

Hall of Happiness and Longevity (Leshou Tang), where the Empress Dowager slept. The curtained bed, the lamps and most of the furniture are original.

Midway along the Long Corridor at the foot of Longevity Hill is the Hall of Dispelling Clouds (Pai Yun Dian), where Cixi held her birthday parties. This hall now houses a collection of birthday gifts, including the portrait of the Empress Dowager painted by Holland's Hubert Vos upon the occasion of her 70th birthday in 1905. The Long Corridor ends at the Pavilion for Listening to the Orioles (Tingli Guan), where there is now a restaurant serving Qing Dynasty imperial dishes.

Just beyond this point is the most famous (or perhaps notorious) monument in the Summer Palace, the **Marble Boat**, known officially as the Boat of Purity and Ease. To Beijingers, it is China's 'ship of fools'. Rebuilt with lavish materials (stone and stained glass) by the Empress Dowager in 1893, this 36-m (118-ft) statue of a boat was restored (it is said) with funds meant to shore up China's woeful navy; it was not long before Japan humiliated China in battles at sea. Cixi's profligate ways, as well as her Machiavellian rise from concubine to Empress, have been popularly held to be the cause of China's weakness and the fall of the last dynasty. The Summer Palace remains as visible testimony to the extravagance of the late Qing Dynasty at the expense of China's freedom and prosperity at the beginning of the 20th century.

Even today the view of Longevity Hill and its scores of tile-roofed pavilions and towers, enjoyed from a pleasure barge drifting across Lake Kunming, is a scene from a dream of old China in which emperors and empresses led lives in gardens of unimaginable splendour. Here even the bridges – connecting lake isles to the palace shores – wouldn't be out of place in a Ming or Qing scroll painting, particularly the celebrated **Seventeen-Arch Bridge** (Shiqi Kong Qiao), 150m (492ft) long and built of white marble.

A short distance from the New Summer Palace is the site of the **Old Summer Palace** (Yuanmingyuan; daily summer 7am–6.30pm, winter 7am–5pm; charge). After its destruction in 1860 by French and British troops, it was left to decay and the court's attention turned to restoring the New Summer Palace. All that's left now are some of the most haunting ruins in China, particularly in a section known as the Garden of Eternal Spring (Changchun Yuan), where European-style halls, marble fountains, mazes and a concert stand are now a broken jumble of ornately carved columns and arches. Every few years there are fresh announcements that the Old Summer Palace will be restored to its former glories. For now, it provides quiet picnic grounds amid the ruins of an empire.

The Marble Boat is a symbol of imperial extravagance

Western Hills

When China's rulers really wanted to escape the heat of the city, they went further west than the Summer Palace to the **Western Hills** (Xishan), romantically known today as **Fragrant Hills Park** (Xiangshan Gongyuan; daily 6am–6pm, until 9pm in summer; charge). Imperial villas first dotted these hillsides – 27km (17 miles) from Beijing – more than 800 years ago. But it was the Qing Emperor Qianlong who converted the Western Hills into a formal mountain retreat for the enjoyment of the court, complete with its own temples, lakes, gardens and even a zoo. Late autumn is the favourite season for park visitors these days, when leaves turn a fiery red. However, locals as well as tourists come to the Western Hills year round for the natural beauty and historic sites.

Gilded *luohans* in the Temple of the Azure Clouds

Two renowned temples still survive in the Western Hills. Near the park's north gate are the four great halls of the **Temple of the Sleeping Buddha** (Wofosi; daily 8am–4pm; charge). In the final hall (Wofodian) there is a 5-m (16-ft) lacquered statue of a reclining Buddha (dating from 1321) about to attain nirvana.

Inside the park's north gate is a larger complex, the **Temple of the Azure Clouds** (Biyunsi; daily 8am–4pm; charge), which is built on the hillside. The body of Sun Yat-sen, founder of the modern Chinese Republic, once lay in state here before it was taken to Nanjing; his hat, coat and coffin are still at this temple.

Located in one of the temple's western courtyards is the fascinating **Hall of 500 Luohan**. *Luohans* are followers of Buddha who achieve enlightenment but choose to stay on Earth to show others the way. The 508 *luohans* portrayed in the

Fragrant Hills Park in autumn

hall's gilded wood figures range from the ecstatic to the gruesome, from the common to the surreal.

Topping the temple is the marble **Diamond Throne Pagoda** (Jinggangbaozuota), built in 1748 under the rule of Emperor Qianlong in the Indian style, with four pagodas and two *stupas* surrounding a 35-m (115-ft) white pagoda.

The most popular site in the Western Hills is natural: a summit known as **Incense Burner Peak** (Xianglufeng), named after the image created when fog comes sweeping over it. A winding path, known as Guijianchou ('Even the Devil is Terrified'), goes to the top, as well as a chair lift (20 minutes each way). At the 557-m (1,827-ft) summit there are pavilions, vendors and small paths into surrounding forests. There are also fine views of the lakes, temples, pavilions and pagodas dotted below, which can be explored upon return. On a clear day, it is tempting to linger. Up here, there's an emperor's view to the southeast, commanding both the pavilions of the Summer Palace and the skyscrapers of Beijing.

Western Temples

About 45km (28 miles) west of the city centre, two ancient temples lie in a delighful rural setting. Beijing's oldest Buddhist temple, **Tanzhesi** (Temple of the Poor and the Mulberry Tree; daily 8am–5pm; charge), was built between AD265 and 316 on terraces carved in dense woods – both Buddhists and Daoists traditionally withdraw to such beautiful places to meditate. The temple is made up of three parts set along a north–south line across the hill slope.

Above the Daxiongbaodian Hall (the main hall) are legendary beasts, sons of the Dragon King, who are supposed to have captured a monk and chained him to the roof. There is a great view of Tanzhesi and its surroundings from here.

In the eastern part of the grounds are a white *dagoba* dating from 1427, two groups of 12th-century pagodas, a bamboo grove and the Pavilion of the Moving Cup (Liubeige),

Lined with stone lions, the Marco Polo Bridge

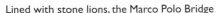

where Qianlong stayed during his visits to the temple.

Equally peaceful is **Jietaisi** (Ordination Terrace Temple; daily 8am–5pm; charge), 8km (5 miles) to the southeast, at the foot of Ma'anshan Hill. This imposing temple dates from 622 and owes its name to the three-level stone terraces surroun-

Transport options

Tanzhesi and Jietaisi can both be reached by bus 931 from Pingguoyuan, or by tourist bus 7 from Qianmen in central Beijing (April to October; departures from 6.30–8.30am only). The easy option is to hire a taxi for the day.

ded by statues, where the dedication ceremony of monks took place. There is not much to be seen inside the temple, but it's worth taking a walk in the grounds.

Marco Polo Bridge

The **Marco Polo Bridge** (Lugouqiao; daily 7am–7pm; charge) is 15km (9 miles) southwest of central Beijing. The Italian merchant Marco Polo, who stayed at the court of the Mongol emperor, Kublai Khan, in the 13th century, wrote so admiringly of the bridge that it became associated with his name. The original 'Lugou' means 'Black Ditch', and is an earlier name for the Yongding River, which flows under the bridge. The first crossing was built here in 1189, improved in 1444 and rebuilt following a flood in 1698. At each end is a 5-m (15-ft) stele; one records the rebuilding of the bridge in the 17th century; the other is inscribed: 'The moon at daybreak over the Lugou Bridge'.

The bridge gained notoriety as the spot where the Japanese invasion of Asia was triggered in World War II. On 7 July 1937, Japanese troops attacked it and the Chinese guards fired back. This provided a pretext for further aggression. By August, China and Japan were at war. A **memorial museum** (same hours as bridge, separate charge) tells the story.

EXCURSIONS

The Great Wall is China's most popular attraction. From Beijing, splendid sections of the wall can be enjoyed at several locations. Less crowded are two of China's greatest imperial cemeteries: the Ming Tombs and the Eastern Qing Tombs. Two more excursions are the Peking Man Museum at Zhoudian and the vast imperial retreat and temples of Chengde.

Great Wall

Construction on the Great Wall began as long ago as the 5th century BC; it winds across northern China for over 10,000km (6,200 miles). However, the **Great Wall** (Wan Li Chang Cheng) that most visitors see consists of a few beautifully restored segments near Beijing that were built, extended or refortified during the Ming Dynasty (AD1368–1644). The Ming builders were the first to finish these massive earthen fortifications with brick. They built a new section of the wall running for 630km (390 miles) just north of Beijing as a massive buffer and early warning system against invaders from the north. This stratagem was to fail, as the Manchus eventually broke through, overthrew the Ming, seized Beijing and established the Qing Dynasty in 1644 – China's last imperial line.

The Great Wall snakes across craggy peaks and deep ravines

Hundreds of thousands of labourers were conscripted over the centuries to extend and repair the Great Wall, and many of them lie buried in its ruins. In the 7th century AD over a million workers were said to be involved in this project, but in the centuries since – until the Ming Dynasty – much of the wall fell into ruin. Even today, most of its length has not been maintained, the earthen remnants barely visible. While it is often reported that the Great Wall is the only manmade object visible from the moon, the claim is dubious at best. Still, it is China's grandest achievement, on a par with Egypt's pyramids and a handful of other ancient wonders of the world.

The Great Wall is best appreciated at four main sites north of Beijing: Badaling, Mutianyu, Juyongguan and Simatai. Three of these four segments have been carefully refurbished, with the fourth, Simatai, largely untouched since the days of the early Ming Dynasty. The earthen foundations of the wall and watchtowers, as well as much of the brickwork, are original, most of it 300 to 500 years old, although extensive remodelling and fresh materials have been added.

The look and the feel are authentic enough, once you are on the wall itself, out of sight of the shops, vendors, tour buses, car parks and cable cars below. The hordes of tourists are another modern addition, of course, but it is possible at all these sites to walk beyond the crowds. The steep mountain scenery is spectacular and the air is usually quite clear. The sheer steepness of the wall's stone stairs and the precarious footing provided by the irregular treads are what first-

Security guard at Badaling

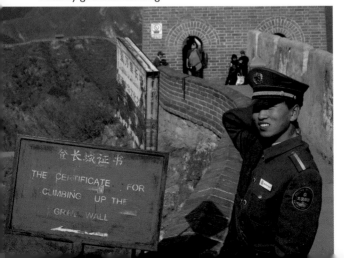

time visitors find most surprising. As it snakes up and down the peaks and ridges, the wall conforms to a challenging topography, one that leaves many tourists gasping for breath. But the views from China's ancient Dragon of Stone make the journey unforgettable.

Badaling

Carefully restored in 1957, the Great Wall at **Badaling**, 67km (42 miles) northwest of Beijing, is the most-visited portion of the wall. The mountain setting is spectacular and the wall rises and falls steeply as it winds up and down the ridges. About 7m (24ft) high and 5m (18ft) wide, this Ming Dynasty fortification is built of tamped earth, stone and brick. Beacon towers of stone and brick are mounted at regular intervals. It is possible to walk the stairs of the restored section for about 2km (1½ miles) before reaching the crumbling remains of the original wall on either end.

At the northern terminus, there is a cable car connecting the wall to a car park below. The car parks at the base of the wall are lined with vendors, gift shops, restaurants and other modern-day attractions, including a cinema and, believe it or not, a KFC fast-food outlet.

Mutianyu

Badaling is crowded, especially from June through to September, but it is quite beautiful. Equally attractive is the second most visited section of the Great Wall at **Mutianyu**, 88km (55 miles) northeast of Beijing. Mutianyu was opened to tourists in 1986 to relieve the overcrowding at Badaling. There is also a cable car at Mutianyu, which eliminates the 20-minute hike up to the wall, and at the foot of the wall there is again a village of vendors, shops and cafés.

Mutianyu is one of the oldest restored sections of the Great Wall in the Beijing area and is thought to have been

Cable cars allow swift access to higher sections of the Wall

built under the Ming rulers nearly 500 years ago, who added the high crenellated parapets on both sides.

Visitors can walk well over a kilometre (nearly a mile) along the top of these ramparts from watchtower to watchtower. At either end you can view the crumbling wall disappearing over the horizon, broken but still visible. Surrounded by its renowned green forests and deep, wooded ravines, the Great Wall at Mutianya is a pleasant alternative to Badaling and worth the extra few miles.

Juyongguan

The Great Wall at **Juyongguan**, 58km (36 miles) northwest of Beijing on the way to the Badaling section, is the newest portion of the wall open to tourism (1998) and the nearest to the capital. Juyongguan contains a massive guard tower marking one of the Great Wall's most celebrated mountain passes. This guard tower, built in 1345, is decorated with Buddhist carvings, with inscriptions in Chinese, Tibetan, Sanskrit and languages of the northern tribes. Some of the temples and parks clustered at the pass in the days of the Ming Dynasty have also been restored here. The wall can be walked for 4km (2½ miles) as it winds over the peaks of the Taihang Mountains.

Simatai

The least restored, least crowded major segment of the Great Wall near Beijing is at **Simatai**, 124km (77 miles) northeast of the capital. Not only is Simatai rather far from the capital, it is also relatively uncrowded and unreconstructed. Its stairways and watchtowers resemble those crumbling edifices one can only glimpse from Badaling, Mutianyu and Juyongguan. The natural scenery is dramatic and the ruined state of the wall gives Simatai a romantic feel (although there is a cable car to the top). However, it is also dangerous, with broken stairways leading up some of the 70-degree inclines. Other portions are in such a ruinous state that you have to walk along the outside of the wall on steep, narrow paths, where the footing is sometimes difficult.

From the village at the base of Simatai there is an 800-m (½-mile) gravel path to the first stairway, which skirts the small Simatai Reservoir. The reservoir divides the Simatai wall from another section, known as Jinshanling, which adventurous hikers can also tackle. Simatai consists of 14 beacon towers, each about 400m (¼ mile) apart, which were once used to transmit fire and smoke signals – tower by tower – to the Chinese armies encamped below should an enemy be sighted. The highest of the beacon towers (known as Wangjinglou) stands at an elevation of 986m (3,235ft), affording a grand view southwest towards Beijing. Locals say that the lights of the capital are visible on clear evenings from here.

The guard tower at Juyongguan

Ming Tombs

The valley of the **Ming Tombs** (daily 8am–5.30pm; charge – extra charges apply for some tombs), 50km (31 miles) northwest of Beijing, is the final resting place of 13 of the 16 Ming emperors. Courtyards and elaborate pavilions, similar to those in the Forbidden City, cap underground burial chambers where the emperors were entombed with their empress and concubines.

Here, a Spirit Way (Shendao) 6½km (4 miles) long – the most renowned graveyard entrance in China – forms a grand avenue into the valley. It is lined with arching entrance gates and magnificent stone statues of animals (12 pairs of creatures, including lions and elephants) and court officials (six pairs), dating from 1435. Inside the Dragon Phoenix Gate are the tombs, of which three have been restored and are open to the public.

Huge stone animals line the path to Emperor Yongle's tomb

The tomb of Emperor Yongle (Changling) is the largest, although its underground palace, where the emperor and his empress are buried, has not been opened. Nor have the 16 satellite vaults, where Yongle's concubines are entombed. The massive courtyards and pavilions above Yongle's burial chambers have been restored and they house some of the Ming Tombs' excavated treasures, including imperial armour.

The burial palace of Emperor Wanli (Dingling) honours the 13th Ming emperor, who ruled from 1573 to 1620. His burial vaults, 27m (88ft) below ground, are made of marble and cover 1,200 sq m (13,000 sq ft). His white marble throne, golden crown and red coffin (along with the coffins of his wife and first concubine) remain in the tomb. The Zhaoling tomb is also open but is less impressive.

The Ming Tombs were once a staple of tours to the Great Wall at Badaling, but tourists have seldom been impressed by the site, finding it dank and poorly restored. A more interesting imperial cemetery is the Eastern Qing Tomb site, although it is much further away from Beijing *(see page 76)*.

Peking Man Museum

The **Peking Man Museum** (daily 8.30am–4.30pm; charge) is 50km (31 miles) southwest of Beijing in the village of Zhoukoudian, whose name has become synonymous with Chinese palaeontology. In 1929, in the hills and caves of Zhoukoudian archaeologists found the skull of a new ancestral link to mankind, *Homo erectus pekinensis* – Peking Man. This discovery suggested that man's closest ancestor might have lived in Asia as well as Africa. Excavations continued until 1937, when most of the fossils were carried out of war-torn China by foreigners, never to return.

The cave on Dragon Bone Hill, where Peking Man lived 690,000 years ago, showed evidence of a community numbering up to 40 individuals. Nearby caves contained fossils

Peking Man Cave

and artefacts from more recent Stone Age settlements (20,000 to 50,000 years ago). These caves may now be visited, their treasures housed in the nearby Peking Man Museum. Here there are moulds of the missing skulls, an array of stone tools, the bones of prehistoric beasts, some human fossils and a modern statue of Peking Man himself.

Eastern Qing Tombs

Nearly as vast and monumental as the Forbidden City, the **Eastern Qing Tombs** (Qingdongling; daily 8.30am–5pm; charge), 125km (78 miles) northeast of Beijing, require a considerable daytrip to view. The journey over country roads, while scenic, is slow. Emperor Shunzhi (1644–61), the founder of the Qing Dynasty, selected this remote spot in a large valley in the mountains while out on a hunting expedition. It is China's largest royal cemetery, with the tombs of five emperors, 15 empresses and over 100 members of the Qing court. Three of China's most famous rulers are buried here: Emperor Qianlong (1711–1799), Emperor Kangxi (1654–1722) and Empress Dowager Cixi (1835–1908).

Like the Ming Tombs, the Eastern Qing Tombs are entered via a long Sacred Way, lined with stone animals and court officials. The oldest tomb (Xiaoling) belongs to Shunzhi and is unopened, but you can visit the 28 pavilions and halls. The tomb of Emperor Kangxi (Jingling) is also unopened, but its magnificent above-ground halls contain many original imperial treasures, including Kangxi's Dragon Throne. The tomb of Emperor Qianlong (Yuling) is open 54m (177ft) underground and it consists of nine immense vaults and the marble coffins of the Manchu emperor and his five favourite consorts.

The most lavish tomb is that of Empress Dowager Cixi. Above her underground palace, inside a sacrificial hall, is a wax museum showing Cixi in full regalia as Goddess of Mercy (her favourite Buddhist deity). The underground palace contains her gold-and-lacquer coffin. Unfortunately, the coffin was desecrated in 1928 by a warlord who also plundered the tomb's treasures, including 25,000 pearls and a burial quilt studded with rare pearls. Many of the treasures

A Royal Rebuff

When Lord George Macartney visited China in 1793 in an attempt to open up normal trade relations between Britain and China, Emperor Qianlong received him at Chengde (see page 78). The meeting took place in the royal audience tent where Macartney was treated to a banquet so splendid he likened it to the 'celebration of a religious mystery'.

However, although the audience seemed to have gone well, it was followed by Qianlong's famous letter to King George in which he praised the king for inclining himself 'towards civilisation', but informed him that 'we have never valued ingenious articles, nor do we have the slightest need of your country's manufactures. Therefore, O King, as regards your request to send someone to remain at the capital, while it is not in harmony with the regulations of the Celestial Empire we also feel very much that it is of no advantage to your country. Hence we have issued these detailed instructions and have commanded your tribute envoys to return safely home. You, O King, should simply act in conformity with our wishes by strengthening your loyalty and swearing perpetual obedience so as to ensure that your country may share the blessings of peace.'

Beijing to Chengde

There are several trains daily from Beijingzhan to Chengde, generally taking approximately 4½ hours – although some take much longer. Buses and minibuses depart from Deshengmen, Dongzhimen and Xizhimen bus stations.

survived, however, and are now on display in the galleries above her tomb.

Chengde

The small city of **Chengde**, 250km (155 miles) northeast of Beijing, requires an overnight stay for visitors based in the capital. But it's well worth a visit in order to view the beautiful palaces and gardens of the imperial resort on the northern edge of the town.

The Qing rulers never forgot their nomadic Manchu roots, and Emperor Kangxi developed this remote valley in the countryside as a summer court and hunting ground in 1703. Construction continued through most of the reign of Kangxi's grandson, Emperor Qianlong. The result is the largest imperial residence in China that has survived in its original condition. It was here that Qianlong received the first official delegation from the West ever to visit China in 1793 *(see page 77)*.

Bishu Shangzhuang (The Mountain Resort for Escaping the Heat; daily 8am–5pm; charge) is surrounded by a 9½-km (6-mile) wall and its grounds comprise the largest surviving imperial garden in China. Among the palaces and halls still in place are the Front Palace, where the emperors conducted official court business, and nine courtyard halls in plain, rustic style. Beyond is a large park with lakes, bridges, pavilions, rockeries and the grasslands and hills where the court enjoyed sports on horseback. There are copies of famous Chinese gardens here, as well as small temples and multi-level viewing pavilions.

Chengde's other main attractions are the temples in the hills outside the park. Many of these '**Eight Outer Temples**' have a strong Tibetan flavour. All were built under the reign of Emperor Qianlong between 1713 and 1779. The Mount Sumera Temple of Happiness and Longevity (Xumifushoumiao) commemorates the Panchen Lama's visit to Chengde in 1779. A copy of the Lama's residence in Shigatse, Tibet, it is crowned by a pagoda decorated in green and yellow tiles. The Small Potala Temple (Putuozongsheng Miao), built in 1769, is even larger and more lavish, covering 22 hectares (54 acres). Its great red hall evokes the Potala Palace in Lhasa, and the arcades within are filled with Buddhist treasures, including sensual figures related to the esoteric Buddhism of the Red Hat sect.

Beyond these and the other temples is **Hammer Rock** (Bangchui Shan), a massive stone pinnacle that can be reached by ski lift or hiking trails. The view from this 18-m (60-ft) natural tower of the valley below, the imperial park and the surrounding Buddhist temples reveals the wealth and scale of the Qing Dynasty at its height. In 1820 this imperial summer villa was all but abandoned after Emperor Jiaqing was killed here by a bolt of lightning. Less than a century later, the Qing Dynasty itself was destroyed by Republican forces, ending China's last period of imperial rule.

The Chengde palaces

WHAT TO DO

Beijing is very different from how it was in the days of Chairman Mao. The past decade has transformed the capital into a 21st-century city with the upmarket shopping malls, restaurants and dynamic nightlife of a fully fledged modern metropolis. But despite these international influences, Beijing has maintained its strong Chinese characteristics, making it a very interesting and distinctive place to visit.

ENTERTAINMENT

From traditional Chinese entertainment to modern Western music, Beijing offers a fairly full calendar of events for visitors, headlined by performances of the Beijing Opera and China's best acrobatic troupes. Your hotel concierge or tour desk has current schedules and can book tickets for you. Traditional teahouse theatres offer an intriguing mix of entertainment, tea and snacks. The capital also has plush cocktail lounges and hardcore dance clubs.

Beijing Opera and Acrobatics

Beijing Opera (Jing Ju) today varies little from the form it took during the Qing Dynasty some 250 years ago. The costumes, choreography, instruments and singing – all unique to China – might seem strange to Westerners, but these highly stylised elements are part of a familiar tradition that many Beijingers love. Other areas of China have their own regional styles of opera, but Beijing Opera is definitely the most famous.

Chinese opera becomes more comprehensible and enjoyable when the plot is known (it's usually a historic drama

Colourful and stylised – Beijing Opera

What's on?

Regular Beijing listing magazines *Time Out Beijing*, *That's Beijing* and *City Weekend* all have useful guides to entertainment, what's on and venue addresses in Chinese and English. You can also visit the websites www.xianzai.com, www.cityweekend.com.cn and www.thebeijinger.com.

or tragic love story) and when subtitles (in English) are projected on a side-screen. It is also helpful to know that the masks, painted faces and costumes identify each character's social role and personality, and that the music, with gongs and cymbals, acts like a film score to emphasise the action on stage.

The best places to take in an evening of opera Beijing-style are the centuries-old Zhengyici Theatre (in the *hutong* directly south of the Hepingmen Quanjude duck restaurant), an opera venue since 1713, and the Liyuan Theatre in the Qianmen Hotel (175 Yong'an Lu). Here spirited excerpts from three or four operas are performed most nights, with English subtitles provided (as well as a choice of snacks).

Other opera theatres of high repute include the Chang'an Grand Theatre (7 Jianguomenwai Dajie) and the Huguang Guildhall (3 Hufang Qiao), which has a history of over 200 years. Admission prices vary widely depending on the seat and snack or meal options, ranging from as little as 20 yuan to over 200 yuan.

Acrobatics are part of most opera performances, but this 2,000-year-old tradition in China has produced its own highly entertaining performers. Some of the best acrobatic groups are based in Beijing. When not touring, the Beijing Acrobatic Troupe performs at the Wansheng Theatre (95 Tianqiao Market). The Sichuan Acrobatic Troupe often uses the Chaoyang Theatre, and the Chinese National Troupe performs at the Universe Theatre (10 Dongzhimen Nan Dajie).

Teahouses

To see snatches of China's traditional performing arts in a setting appropriate for an imperial banquet, try one of Beijing's special teahouses. At these intimate dinner theatres, decorated in Qing Dynasty fashion (carved wood trim, paper lanterns and red columns), you can enjoy a local snack or full Chinese meal while watching a variety of acts on stage, including opera highlights, acrobatics, magic shows, ethnic dancing, puppetry, storytelling and comedy.

The two top teahouse theatres in the capital are the Laoshe Teahouse (3 Qianmenxi Dajie), with nightly variety shows and snacks, and the Tianqiao Happy Teahouse (113 Tianqiao Market), where the staff are dressed in Qing costumes.

Expert teas in a teahouse

Nightlife

The main bar areas are Sanlitun, Jianguomenwai/Workers' Stadium, the Back Lakes and Weigongcun in the Haidian university district.

Much of Beijing's contemporary music scene is centred in the Sanlitun area, a favourite of expatriates and foreign visitors looking for comfortable bars and late-night international cafés. Local Chinese also frequent these spots, where the live music ranges from rock to jazz. Prices for drinks (especially for imported wines, spirits and beers) are high for

Beijing but are on a par with those in the West. Sanlitun Lu features several dozen café bars in the space of a few blocks.

Among the most popular Western-style pubs are The Tree (behind the Youyi Youth Hostel, to the west of Sanlitun Bar Street), which is popular for its pizzas and Belgian beers; The Rickshaw (on Sanlitun South Street), which has filling Mexican food and cheap beers; and Frank's Place (west of Rosedale Hotel in the Lido Area), a legend among expats. Frank's Place, The Rickshaw and The Pavilion – a bar with a garden on Workers' Stadium West Road – all have big-screen sports.

For live jazz the best place in town is the East Shore Live Jazz Café, beautifully located on the banks of Qianhai opposite Lotus Lane. Get here before 9pm to ensure a seat. You can also hear jazz at the slightly stuffy CD Jazz Café (Nongzhanguan, Third Ring Road East) or Jazz Ya (18 Sanlitun Lu), a Japanese eatery that occasionally has live bands.

The Workers' Stadium is clubbing central. Cargo and Coco Banana line its West Road and face the capital's only gay club, Destination. Inside the Workers' Stadium complex you'll find Beijing's most popular club, Mix, which plays R'n'B, and its flashier sister, Remix. White Rabbit (on Lucky Street near Chaoyang Park) is the nearest thing to a good London club while Star Live (Tango outside Ditan Park South Gate) is the best venue for live bands. There's a recent trend for flashy, very expensive bar–lounges. Block 8 (Chaoyang Park West Gate) is the leader of the pack, and 1949: The Hidden City, near Sanlitun South Street, has more of the same.

Karaoke bar in East Beijing

Chinese warriors at the Panjiayuan Market

SHOPPING

Beijing has some of the world's best places to shop for Chinese-made goods and traditional arts and crafts, often with prices far below those paid in the West. It is renowned for its selection of silk fabrics and clothing, embroidery, pearls, jade, porcelains, cloisonné, lacquerware, carpets, furniture, antiques and artwork (contemporary and traditional).

The most popular shopping streets are Wangfujing Dajie, Liulichang Culture Street and Dazhalan Jie south of Tiananmen Square, and Xidan Street west of the city centre (a locals' favourite), which are superb for window-shopping. Some English is spoken in most shops, which open daily from about 9am to 8pm or later. Sunday is the most crowded day to shop. Few stores accept credit cards, so carry plenty of Chinese cash.

The Friendship Store, a comprehensive department store for tourists, east of the Forbidden City (at 17 Jianguomenwai

Dajie), gives a good idea of the goods available in Beijing and what they should cost (essentially less than what the Friendship Store is asking). The best places to find bargains are street markets and bazaars, which are also the most interesting, although their numbers are dwindling as Beijing modernises.

Best Buys

Antiques. Beijing has antiques galore – and plenty of fakes, too. Objects dating before 1840 cannot be exported. Hotel shops and the Friendship Store are the most reliable antiques dealers, and they often provide international shipping services for purchases. The antiques shops along Liulichang Culture Street are worth looking at, as is the Panjiayuan Market on Sunday mornings *(see page 90)*.

Art. Contemporary art galleries can be found in the Wangfujing area and in some of the leading hotels (notably China World and Holiday Inn Crowne Plaza). Reproductions of classic and traditional landscapes and Chinese masterpieces are sold at most galleries, as are low-priced painted scrolls. The Dashanzi Factory 798 district is the hip place to go for galleries showing contemporary art.

The Four Treasures of the Study

Writing and painting materials are referred to in China as the Four Treasures of the Study, consisting of the brush, ink stick, rubbing stone and paper. Such tools have long been held in high esteem by Chinese poets, scholars and painters; there are reliable records which show that brush and ink were being used as early as the 1st century BC, during the Han period. Chinese ink was only taken up in Europe as a distinct kind of paint in the 17th century. The attractive shops along Liulichang *(see page 50)* are the best places in Beijing to buy traditional brushes, paper, ink sticks, rubbing stones and other artists' materials.

Arts and crafts. Traditional handmade items include paper kites and fans, ceramic teapots, bamboo knick-knacks, lacquerware, chopsticks and cloisonné bracelets. Cheap to buy, such items are widely available in department stores and from vendors at tourist sites.

Carpets. Handmade carpets from the far western provinces and from Tibet are popular in Beijing. Those made of silk or wool should be inspected carefully. The

Chinese calligraphy

colours should not be fading and the threads should be fine and tightly woven. Begin shopping at the Friendship Store or the Beijing Carpet Import and Export Corporation in the Hong Kong Macao Centre (Third Ring Road East).

Cashmere. Department stores and clothing outlets in shopping plazas sell well-made wool and cashmere garments in Western sizes much cheaper than at home.

Chops (seals). Everyone who was anyone in China had their own carved stamp, called a *chop*, usually a palm-sized stone block that was dipped in a special red ink and used as an official signature and seal. *Chops* are still used widely today. At the Friendship Store, in the markets and in some hotels, master carvers can quickly create a *chop* with your name on it in any language, including Chinese characters.

Collectables. Nearly every open market, street stall and alley bazaar sells collectables for which you must bargain. Mao buttons and posters, old Chinese coins, Buddhist statues, wood carvings and handpainted plates are all popular.

Jade. Buy only what you like at a price you can easily afford. Some jade is fake. Colour, transparency, smoothness and cut determine price. Check prices at the Friendship Store first.

Pearls. These can be a very good buy in Beijing. The third floor of the Hongqiao Market *(see page 91)* is the leading outlet for freshwater and saltwater pearls, with prices ranging from 20 to 20,000 yuan. Look for uniformity in the size, shape and colour of pearls. The best ones are large and highly lustrous.

Porcelain. The most famous hand-painted porcelain is Jingdezhen and the best choice is found at the Friendship Store.

Silk and embroidery. The Friendship Store, department stores, hotel and silk shops carry good selections of silk fabrics and garments in Western sizes. They also sell inexpensive embroidered goods, such as tablecloths and sheets. Try the Yuanlong Embroidery and Silk Store at the south entry to the Temple of Heaven.

Embroidered boots

Tea. Small tea shops along Wangfujing and Liulichang streets sell loose-leaf green teas and teaware. Good outlets include the Jiguge Teahouse at 132 Liulichang Dongjie and Bichu Tea Shop at 233 Wangfujing Dajie.

Malls and Plazas

The Friendship Store on east Chang'an Avenue and the Beijing Department Store (255 Wangfujing Dajie), once purveyors of Beijing's most up-to-date fashions and top merchandise, have been superseded by the sudden eruption of huge Westernised shopping malls and plazas. Boutiques with an international flair, designer-label outlets, speciality shops, fast-food restaurants, supermarkets, department stores and cinemas have all gathered under single roofs. Although the prices are high

All kinds of Chinese kitsch are available at outdoor markets

by local standards and much of the merchandise is imported, you can still find bargains.

Beijing's premier mega-malls can be found along Wangfujing Street. The vast malls at the **Oriental Plaza** and the six-storey **Sun Dong An Plaza** together feature hundreds of shops ranging from a Chinese supermarket and silk and clothing outlets to McDonald's and London Fog. The **Xidan** shopping district, about 2km (1½ miles) west of the Forbidden City, and the **Beijing New World Centre** by Chongwenmen also host massive shopping centres to rival those of Wangfujing.

The **Friendship Shopping City** at the Lufthansa Centre serves those staying at the international hotels in northeast Beijing on the Third Ring Road. **China World Trade Centre**'s shopping plaza (at 1 Jianguomenwai Dajie) includes an ice-skating rink, an internet café and China's first Starbucks coffee shop. New top-end shopping malls dripping with Gucci, Cartier and Dolce & Gabbana include Shin Kong Place (Dawang Lu, east of the central business district), Season's Place on Financial Street with its Lane Crawford department store, and Park Life in the central business district's Yintai Centre.

Markets and Bazaars

Beijing's open-air markets are disappearing as the city modernises, a number of them having been (permanently) closed or otherwise relegated to indoor spaces. Nevertheless, they can still offer the most interesting shopping ventures in the capital. Bargaining is the rule. The vendors are experts, language presents no barrier and buyers should exercise patience and caution. It helps to have a notion of the market value of the merchandise by first checking out prices in the Friendship Store. Street markets should have the lowest prices, but the initial price will always be on the high side.

The **Panjiayuan Market** (also known as the Dirt Market or Ghost Market) is the most interesting. Lying at the southeast corner of the Third Ring Road, it goes into full swing at sunrise every Sunday morning, when over 100,000 visitors sift through wares ranging from antiques and collectables to

A souvenir shop inside the old railway station at Qianmen

ceramics and family heirlooms. Bargaining is expected and patience required; also watch out for pickpockets. The best time to go is early morning or at lunchtime when the crowds thin out (it begins to shut down by mid-afternoon). Just to the south is **Beijing Curio City**, a four-storey complex with a huge range of antiques. Prices are a little higher here.

The **Ritan Office Building Market** at 15 Guanghua Lu, near the south gate of Ritan Park, sells clothing,

Pirates

China is expert at making pirated goods, and authorities have paid lip service to stamping out the practice. Fake designer handbags, jewellery, sportswear, and other clothing are sold at the Silk Street and Yashow Markets. The Silk Street Markets, apparently not recognising the irony, have released their own Silk Street brand, and warned counterfeiters that pirating their designs would have serious consequences.

jewellery, shoes and some knick-knacks. This is a good place to buy the works of local designers who merge Chinese and Western styles and international name-brand clothes that have been rejected for export. The **Hongqiao Market**, on the northeast edge of the Temple of Heaven Park, is the best place for jewellery bargains, especially pearls. It also sells a bewildering variety of food, electronics, clothes and antiques. **Ya Show Sanlitun Clothing Market**, on Gongtibei Lu near Sanlitun, sells just about everything a tourist in Beijing might want to buy. It is open 10am–8pm daily.

One market that still offers something unique is **Guanyuan**. Specialising in wildlife, curious visitors are attracted by the colourful birds in long rows of cages, either piled on top of each other or hanging from poles and branches. On the western side of the market, which is near Fuchengmen, are brilliantly coloured ornamental fish swimming in huge glass containers or small enamel bowls.

SPORTS

The host city of the 2008 Olympics offers a variety of recreational activities, though most visitors do not come to Beijing for outdoor pursuits or sports. Most international hotels maintain full-service fitness centres with exercise machines, saunas, indoor swimming pools and other facilities such as tennis courts, with day rates for non-guests. The city parks are fine places for jogging, exercises, *tai chi,* walking and other early-morning workouts. Golf, bowling and billiards are three of the most popular recreational sports.

Dongdan Sports Centre (Dongdan Dajie, near Chang'an Dajie) has a swimming pool, indoor tennis and squash courts and other facilities right in the city centre, and the China World Hotel has indoor tennis courts. There are two massive outdoor swimming pools just inside the south gate of

Tai chi in the Temple of Heaven Park

the Workers' Stadium (Gongren Tiyuchang Nanmen). Beijing also offers bungee jumping (at the Shidu Bungee Jumping Facility in the Fangshan District), paintball (at the Olympic Sports Centre Paintball Strike Range in Chaoyang), rock climbing (at the Qidagudu Climbing Club in the Xuanwu District) and horseback riding (at the Equuleus Riding Club, off Jingshun Lu). The High Club (www.highclub.cn), organises horse-riding day trips in the Kanxi grasslands 80km (50 miles) northwest of Beijing.

Golf. Beijing's top course is the Beijing International Golf Club, located near the Ming Tombs. The Beijing Grand Canal Golf Club, east of Beijing, has night golf. Near the airport, the Beijing Country Golf Club provides 36 holes. One of the newest championship golf courses, designed by Graham Marsh, is the Huatang International Golf Course. The closest course to the city is the Chaoyang Golf Club, a nine-hole course with a driving range. All these courses are open to the public (make reservations through your hotel), and they rent clubs and provide caddies.

Bowling. Modern bowling lanes enjoyed a boom in Beijing during the 1990s, with alleys located in the Holiday Inn Lido, Beijing International and other hotels, including the China World Hotel.

Ice skating. Beihai Park and the Summer Palace both offer superb outdoor ice skating in the winter, with skate rental at stalls on the shoreline. Indoor skating is available at the Ditan Ice Arena in Ditan Park and at the underground shopping centre connecting the Traders and China World hotels (1 Jianguomenwai Dajie).

Spectator sports. Football (soccer) has overtaken basketball as the most popular spectator sport in China. Beijing's two professional teams, Beijing Guo'an (football) and the Beijing Ducks (basketball), play at the Workers' Stadium in northeast Beijing.

ACTIVITIES FOR CHILDREN

Beijing has dozens of attractions for children. There's the Beijing Zoo *(see page 58)*, with its pandas and tigers, and the Beijing Aquarium next door. The Blue Aquarium, at the south gate of the Workers' Stadium, has a long underwater tunnel.

Happy Valley Amusement Park, on the East Fourth Ring Road, is a giant new funfair, the best and most modern in the city. The Beijing Amusement Park (west side of Longtan Lake Park) is the old-fashioned standard, with a Ferris wheel, go-carts and a looping roller coaster. China's largest theme park, World Park, near the Fourth Ring Road in Fangtai, is stocked with scale models of 100 of the world's greatest monuments, landmarks and skylines. Fans of miniature golf can play at Kaite Mini-Golf (north entrance, Ritan Park) and younger kids can let off steam at Fundazzle indoor playground, near the Workers' Stadium on Gongren Tiyuchang Lu.

Puppet shows can sometimes be seen at the China Puppet Theatre (1 Anhuaxili) and kids can dress up as a character from Chinese opera at Fenmo Nong Zhuang (29 Liangmaqiao Lu). The Chinese Culture Club (www.chinesecultureclub.com), offers classes in painting, calligraphy and martial arts.

Kite-flying in Tiananmen Square

Kids with a scientific bent may enjoy the Science and Technology Museum on the north side of the Third Ring Road (1 Beisanhuan Zhong Lu). The Sony Explora Science Centre in the Oriental Plaza (Chaoyang Park) features interactive science and technology exhibits that both entertain and educate.

Calendar of Events

January–February *Lunar New Year* – also called 'Spring Festival' – is China's biggest celebration, held on the first day of the lunar calendar (it usually falls in late January or early February). On the first three days all offices, banks and many shops are closed. Parks, temples and markets hold special celebrations all over the capital and families get together to exchange gifts and eat large meals. An ice-sculpture display is held at Longqingxia Park. Festivities can last for 15 days.

February The *Lantern Festival* falls exactly 15 days after the Lunar New Year, on the first full moon. Parks and temples display decorative paper lanterns and hold celebrations punctuated by fireworks and dances.

April–May Taking place during April is the *Qingming Festival*, also known as the Festival of Light or Grave-Sweeping Day, when families visit the graves of ancestors offering food and wine, and burning 'spirit money'. On *International Workers' Day* on 1 May, most places are closed except restaurants and major sights.

June–July The *Dragon Boat Festival* occurs on the fifth day of the fifth lunar month. Dragon boat races are held in Beijing at the Chinese Cultural Park (1 Minzu Lu), and people eat *zongzi*, a sticky rice ball wrapped in bamboo leaves.

September *Moon Festival*, or Mid-Autumn Festival, celebrates the harvest moon and a revolt against Mongol rule in the 14th century. Held on the 15th day of the eighth lunar month, everyone eats moon cakes (sweet biscuits with red bean, bean curd, sesame, or date paste).

October *National Day*, held on the first day of October, commemorates the founding of the People's Republic of China on 1 October 1949. The largest National Day celebration is in Beijing at Tiananmen Square, where a patriotic rally fills the square and nearby streets. The *Beijing International Marathon* takes place in the third week of October.

October–November The *Red Leaf Festival* is held at the Fragrant Hills Park in the Western Hills, when the autumn leaves change colour, and the park's markets and temples hold celebrations. In mid-November, the *China International Jazz Festival* is staged throughout Beijing.

EATING OUT

Beijing offers a sumptuous banquet of eating choices unrivalled in variety by any other city in China. Every regional cuisine – from Sichuan to Cantonese – is well represented among the capital's restaurants, headlined by such Beijing specialities as Beijing duck, Northern China pastries, Mongolian hot pots and imperial dishes prepared according to recipes once used in the Forbidden City. Beijing also offers a full range of international and Western-style restaurants, both inside and outside its major hotels. The preferred dishes of many Beijingers (for low price as much as for taste) consist of local favourites prepared by vendors who line streets, alleys and night markets with their small, blazing coal-burning stoves.

About chopsticks

Chopsticks, or *kuaizi*, date back thousands of years. Although bone, ivory, gold, jade and steel have all been used, most chopsticks are now made of wood and are thrown away after each meal.

When and How to Eat

Meals are a primary concern of Beijingers, perhaps the most important events of daily life. Chinese restaurants and cafés keep fairly limited hours, serving breakfast 7am–9am, lunch 11.30am–2pm and dinner 5pm–8pm, although hotels have longer hours (often maintaining 24-hour restaurants). International buffet brunches are popular in hotels on Sundays (11am–3pm). Night markets serve local snacks from dusk to midnight, although there is no assurance of proper hygiene. Café bars in Sanlitun and elsewhere serve Western foods and snacks well into the night.

Chinese cuisine is usually served 'family style', meaning that diners help themselves to each item or course from a single large platter at each table. Chopsticks are the norm (practise at home if possible), but Western-style utensils are becoming quite common in most restaurants that regularly serve foreign visitors, as are English-language menus.

At banquets, service is also 'family style'. The evening's dishes are served one at a time, fresh from the kitchen. Each new dish is placed on a small platform tray that can be rotated by the diners. The host often serves guests with the first sampling from each item, then guests can help themselves.

Rice is normally served at the end of a meal, but guests may request a bowl of steamed rice at any time. Appetisers on small plates come first, followed by a soup and the main entrées. Fruit slices are usually served for dessert. Rice is typically eaten with the bowl held near the mouth; soup may be slurped and noodles may be 'inhaled'.

A night market snack of skewered scorpions

The key element is to enjoy the meal and not to stand on ceremony. Meals are a time for enjoyment and relaxation, although in a traditional banquet there is often no time at the end to converse. The host simply stands up, signalling an abrupt end to the feast.

The Chinese food in Beijing is prepared to local tastes and is quite different in flavour and presentation from that served overseas, being more bold than delicate, more basic than subtle, but usually quite delicious.

A chef preparing noodles

Beijing Cuisine

No Beijing visit is complete without a sampling of the local specialities, especially the famous Beijing duck. Since Beijing is in the north of China and experiences cold weather, it has developed a hearty fare that relies more on bread, noodles, potatoes, cabbage and vinegar than on rice, seafood and chilli sauces. The local food is not known for its fiery seasonings, but garlic, salt, ginger and other pungent spices are common.

Almost as famous in Beijing as Beijing Duck are *jiaozi* (bite-sized steamed dumplings) filled with vegetables, meats or seafood. These resemble what's known in southern China and around the world as *dim sum*. Diners often season them with vinegar and they are available from street-side vendors or at special *jiaozi* restaurants (such as Duyichu on Qianmen Dajie) or as part of a complete dinner with spring rolls and noodles at the Sihexuan Restaurant in the Jinglun Hotel.

Imperial cuisine comes from the recipes developed for the royal court in Beijing's Forbidden City. Elaborate and complex, using exotic ingredients (swan's liver, lake turtles), it survived China's last dynasty, the Qing (1644–1911), and in the hands of former court chefs appeared in some of Beijing's finest restaurants. The Fangshan Restaurant at Beihai Park serves its version of imperial dishes and banquets (using noodles, pork, duck and winter vegetables) in an old mansion. A relative newcomer, the Li Family Restaurant, housed in a traditional courtyard house in a *hutong*, uses the same dynastic recipes and has become the capital's most popular (and difficult-to-book) eating experience.

Cultural Revolution cafés are also trendy newcomers in Beijing, specialising in the simple countryside fare of steamed breads, oily noodles and steamed cabbage that many Beijingers experienced during the bleak years of social upheaval (1966–76). Cafés such as The East is Red (266 Baijiaolou, Chaoyang) and Guoqi Niandai Xiangcai Guan (North Second Ring Road opposite Gulou subway station) have waiting staff clad in Red Army-esque uniforms and Mao posters to get you in the mood.

Beijing Duck

Beijing duck is Beijing's most famous speciality and there are some venerable restaurants that feature this as their mainstay. The duck is roasted whole over an open flame, presented at the table, then carved into small strips. Noted for its crispy skin and fat, the duck is placed on a thin pancake, seasoned with plum sauce and spring onion, rolled up and eaten with the fingers or chopsticks. The Quan Jude chain of duck restaurants has been in business in Beijing for over a century. Full duck banquets don't come cheap; in fact, they are too expensive for most Chinese families and are reserved for special occasions. There are a number of cheaper duck restaurants in Beijing, but sadly many have become pure mass-production centres.

Mongolian hot-pot restaurants are popular all over Beijing, in summer as well as winter. Lamb is the favoured meat, sliced so the diner can dip it into the cauldron of boiling oil in the centre of the table and cook to taste. A variety of other cook-it-yourself items are on hand, including fish, noodles, bean vermicelli, cabbage and potatoes. The nomadic Mongolian tribes to the north introduced this cuisine to the capital, along with the barbecue. Guijie (Ghost Street) just south of the Lama Temple, is wall to wall with hot-pot restaurants that are open until the early hours of the morning.

The **night markets** of Beijing serve up samples of *jiaozi*, noodles and lamb kebabs from their street-side stalls. The largest such market is Dong'anmen, a central street running west from Wangfujing and east of the Forbidden City. Any time of day, street vendors all over Beijing dish up the favourite local snacks, including *baozi* (stuffed steamed buns), *hundun* (won-

Dong'anmen night market offers a wide range of snacks

ton soup), *jian bing guozi* (crepes with hot sauce), *miantiao* (noodles) and *youtiao* (deep-fried dough strands), as well as more exotic fare such as scorpions and other delicacies for the daring.

Regional Cuisine

The most popular regional cuisine in Beijing – and in fact around the world – is **Cantonese**. Known for its seafood, sauces, exotic ingredients (snake, monkey) and such delicacies as shark's fin

A serving of scallops

and bird's-nest soup, southern cooking (including Chaozhou as well as Cantonese) graces some of Beijing's most upscale Chinese restaurants. Notable among these are Summer Palace in the China World Hotel, Shang Palace in the Shangri-La Hotel, Huang Ting in the Peninsula Hotel and Tingliguan, located in an old pavilion at the Summer Palace. There are several good restaurants specialising in the spicier foods of Hunan province and the fruits and vegetables of southwest Yunnan. A popular Cantonese breakfast, *dim sum* is best enjoyed at the award-winning Sampan Restaurant in the Gloria Plaza hotel.

Growing in popularity are Beijing's **Shanghai** restaurants, famed for their freshwater crab, eel, shrimp and fish and rice dishes. The Shanghai Restaurant (Kunlun Hotel) employs Shanghai chefs and ships in fresh, authentic ingredients. **Sichuan** cuisine, with hot chilli-infused dishes and its own version of the hot-pot, also has a large following. The South Beauty restaurant chain serves excellent Sichuan food (try the one in Pacific Century Place on Workers' Stadium North Road).

A seafood spread

Muslim restaurants are also a fixture in Beijing. Muslims, many of them Uighur people from the far-western province of Xinjiang, have their own Beijing neighbourhoods and lively restaurants, featuring dancers and singers as well as mutton shish kebabs and flat breads.

Vegetarian fare is surprisingly spare, but Beijing does have several good restaurants for non-meateaters: Xu Xiang Zhai (26 Guozijian Jie), just east of the Confucius Temple and the venerable Gongdelin (south of Tiananmen Square).

International Restaurants

Excellent international alternatives are easily found, from fine French cooking to Tex-Mex, not only in Beijing's luxury hotels, but in a growing number of excellent independent street cafés. Most feature chefs from abroad.

Diners wanting variety will find no shortage of Malaysian, Thai, Vietnamese, Korean, Indian and other **Asian** restaurants. There are a number of five-star hotels which have Japanese restaurants on their premises, such as Nishimura in the Shangri-La Beijing Hotel.

Superb **French** and **Continental** fare is served by Aria (China World Hotel), Justine's (Jianguo Hotel). Fine fusion food is delivered in The CourtYard, beautifully located overlooking the Forbidden City. German choices include Bavaria Bierstube (Palace Hotel) and Paulaner Brauhaus (Kempinski Hotel). **Italian** dining is quite upscale at Assaggi (Sanlitun) and Cepe (at the Ritz Carlton).

Beijing has some fine South and Central American restaurants. The Brazilian eatery, Alameda (Sanlitun), is everybody's favourite, while for hearty Tex Mex there's Pete's Tex Mex Grill (next to the St Regis Hotel on Jianguomenwai). For fish and chips try Fish Nation (Nanluogu Xiang). Superb American fare is dished out at One East on Third (Beijing Hilton). Indian is another cuisine niche that Beijing has been grooming of late. The Taj Pavilion (Holiday Inn Lido) is considered by some to be the best Indian restaurant in the city, while the cheaper Mirch Masala (Nanluogu Xiang) serves great fresh dishes and the hottest chicken vindaloo in town.

Finally, should you succumb to **fast-food** cravings, Beijing has an abundant supply of burgers, fries, pizzas and chicken seemingly on every corner, with more than 50 McDonald's, 20 KFCs and a smattering of Pizza Huts, as well as outlets for Haagen-Dazs, Dunkin' Donuts and Starbucks.

Fast food is big in Beijing

What to Drink

China invented tea *(cha)* as a beverage and has thousands of years of brewing experience. The light green tea is favoured, although the darker 'red' teas (known in the West as 'black') are sometimes available. Coffee *(kafei)* can be provided at most restaurants, and Western-style coffee houses are starting to catch on. Better restaurants, especially in hotels, brew up lattés and some stronger coffees that are more to Westerners' taste than the watery instant coffee common throughout China.

Bottled water, imported and local, can be purchased at stores and on most street corners. Foreign-brand soft drinks *(qishui)* are a staple at Beijing cafés, grocery stores and street stalls. Coca-Cola *(kekou kele)*, made under licence in Beijing, has long been available in the capital.

A selection of Chinese tea

Beer *(pijiu)* is perhaps the most favoured drink – next to tea – among diners in the city. Imported beers are widely available and micro-breweries are springing up all over, but the most popular beers are China's own Tsing-tao (distributed worldwide) and Beijing's local Yanjing.

China's wine industry is still in its infancy; several Sino-French joint ventures produce passable, inexpensive wine. However, China's *huangjiu* (yellow wine made from corn millet or glutinous rice) has been made for some

4,000 years. It has a high alcohol content, with a sweet and rough taste.

Banquets are routinely interrupted by toasts from small glasses filled with *bai-jiu*, a Chinese 'fire water' made from sorghum. This clear spirit tests the mettle of experienced drinkers and is best in modest amounts.

Western drinks chain with an Eastern flavour

To Help you Order...

I'd like...	**Wǒ yào...**	我要
I'm a vegetarian	**Wǒ shì chī sù de rén**	我是吃素的人
menu	**càidān**	菜单
The bill, please	**Qǐng jié zhàng**	请结帐

...And Read the Menu

beef/pork/lamb	**niú/zhū/yáng**	牛肉/猪肉/羊肉
beer	**píjiǔ**	啤酒
fish	**yú**	鱼
fried rice	**dàn chǎo fàn**	蛋炒饭
fruit	**shuǐguǒ**	水果
hotpot	**huǒ guō**	火锅
noodles	**miàntiáo**	面条
pancakes	**bǐng**	饼
stuffed pasta parcels	**jiǎozi**	饺子
steamed meat buns	**bāozi**	包子
tea	**cháshuǐ**	茶水
vegetables	**shūcài**	蔬菜
won-ton soup	**húndùn**	混沌

HANDY TRAVEL TIPS
An A–Z Summary of Practical Information

A

ACCOMMODATION

About 10 years ago, most Beijing hotels were little more than crash courses in culture shock, in part because China had learned the 'modern' hotel business from the Soviet Union in the 1950s. Today, however, China is learning from the West, and its hotel services and facilities are often of international calibre.

Beijing hotels are graded with one to five stars by the government, with the ratings largely determined by the hotel facilities (that is, by swimming pools rather than by quality of service). One- and two-star hotels are quite basic affairs, often shabby, with indifferent service and no air conditioning. The budget hotels that are officially approved for foreign guests are favoured by adventurous backpackers and those willing to rough it.

Beijing's three-star hotels represent a major step up in comfort and price. They have a range of modern conveniences, including reasonably clean and usually functional private bathrooms, money-exchange and tour counters, business centres, restaurants, satellite TV and a few staff members conversant in English. Service and housekeeping levels are well below those of four- and five-star hotels, however.

Beijing's stable of deluxe accommodation is impressive: almost all four- and five-star hotels are of international level. Some have foreign management teams, particularly those affiliated with international hotel chains (Shangri-La, Hyatt, Holiday Inn, Swissôtel, Radisson, Kempinski, Hilton, Sheraton). The several dozen five-star hotels in the capital are quite grand, but so are their room rates (on a par with fine hotels in Europe and North America). There is quite a big difference in price between the five-star establishments and the many, perfectly comfortable, mid-to-upper-range hotels. There are no B&B or camping options in or near Beijing, but there are plenty of hostels.

From late November through to early April, however, many hotels lower their rates, and competition year round often leads to special rates, particularly when a visitor books ahead (which one must do in May and October, the busiest months). Most business and independent travellers make reservations long before arriving in Beijing. While excellent deals are sometimes offered at the hotel counters in Beijing Capital Airport, counting on last-minute reservations is not for the faint-hearted or the wise traveller. The websites www.elong. net and www.ctrip.com often have good hotel deals.

| Single room | **Dānrén fángjiān** | 单人房间 |
| Double room | **Shuāngrén fángjiān** | 双人房间 |

AIRPORT

Beijing Capital International Airport (www.bcia.com.cn), now sports the newly opened 'dragon-backed' Terminal 3 – the largest airport terminal in the world. Located just 27km (17 miles) northeast of the city centre and connected to Beijing by a fast toll road and a subway line, the airport is about 30–40 minutes from most hotels, but allow one hour in peak periods.

Arrival. Passports (with a China visa) and health and customs forms are required to pass through the immigration and customs checkpoints. The process is usually quick. The arrival hall is always chaotic. Ignore touts hawking taxi rides. Near the exit is a branch of the Bank of China offering currency exchange (6am to midnight daily), as well as automated currency-exchange machines. There are no airport porters, but there are self-service luggage carts.

To reach the centre of Beijing, there are four options. The hotel counters near the main exit provide their own shuttle bus and limousine service (requiring reservations in advance). Air China (www.airchina.com.cn) offers inexpensive coach services from the airport to several stops in the city centre. Destinations include the main Air China booking office on Chang'an Xidajie, close to Xidan; the Lufthansa Centre; and the Beijing International Hotel, north of Beijing railway station (Beijingzhan). Taxis are available at all stops. The third option is an airport taxi. Ignore taxi hustlers, line up in the taxi queue at the kerb and be sure your taxi has a working meter. Depending on the destination and category of taxi, the fare will be between 60 and 120 yuan. The final option is by subway. The new underground line whisks passengers from the terminals to downtown Dongzhimen on the East Second Ring Road in 20 minutes.

Departure. Arrive at least two hours before scheduled departure (as ticket and security queues are long).

B

BICYCLE HIRE

As cars have spilled over into bicycle lanes and air pollution has worsened, the joys of cycling have diminished and its dangers increased. Nonetheless, if you have steady nerves, cycling is a great way to get around and will give you a completely different view of the city. The best option may be to hire a bike in a less crowded district – Sanlitun, the Ritan Park neighbourhood and the Houhai area are good bets – until you are more familiar with the rules of the road. Many hotels and hostels have bicycles for hire, usually for around 20 yuan per day, although it can cost as much as 100 yuan from an upmarket hotel. Check for good brakes, full tyres, a working bell and a functioning bike lock; bikes must be parked in official bike parks, for a minimal charge, available everywhere. *(See page 45)*.

BUDGETING FOR YOUR TRIP

Beijing costs are rising quickly due to inflation and the strengthening yuan. But aside from major fixed expenses such as accommodation, prices are lower than in most Western capitals, except for imported goods and services. The US$ equivalents below are approximate.

Taxi. 15–40 yuan (US$2–7), depending on distance.

Subway. 2 yuan (US$0.35).

Meals. Lunch, if you're eating local, seldom costs more than US$8 and dinner buffets even in expensive hotels can be enjoyed for around US$25. Food from street vendors is much cheaper. Drinks are comparatively expensive, with coffee 20 yuan (US$2.80), soft drinks 10 yuan (US$1.40) and beer in a bar or restaurant 25–50 yuan (US$3.50–7), but tea is often free. Western-style supermarkets stock imported goods at roughly the same prices charged overseas.

Tickets. Admission to the most popular attractions is 10–80 yuan (US$1.40–11). Some places have different prices, depending upon how many areas or exhibitions are to be visited – an all-inclusive ticket is called a *tao piao* and is usually worth buying unless you specifically want to visit one area only.

Guided day tours. 250–400 yuan (US$35–55), often with lunch.

Summary. After budgeting for accommodation, you can expect to spend an additional US$10–$100 per day, depending on what you buy at shops and which restaurants you select.

C

CAR HIRE

Hiring a self-drive car, motorcycle or scooter in Beijing is not an option for tourists because a Chinese driver's licence and residency permit are required. A car with driver rented from an agency such as Hertz costs from US$50 a day; major hotels can rent chauffeured sedans to guests, although the rates start at US$100 per day.

CLIMATE

Beijing is extremely hot and humid in the summer (mid-June–late August), making spring (late April–mid-June) and autumn (September–October) the high tourist seasons. Winters (November–March) are cold, although usually not rainy or snowy, but few tourists visit and many attractions are closed or only partially open. Rains are heaviest in July and August; dust storms are most frequent in March and April. Overall, the best weather conditions are from mid-September to mid-November (which is also when the capital is most crowded with tourists). Beijing's pollution is harrowing.

Approximate monthly average temperatures are as follows:

	J	F	M	A	M	J	J	A	S	O	N	D
°C	-4	-2	4	13	20	25	26	25	20	13	4	-3
°F	25	28	39	55	68	77	79	77	68	55	39	27

CLOTHING

Above all pack a pair of comfortable, durable walking shoes. The pavements take a toll on shoes and the dusty air is hard on clothing. Cotton shirts and trousers are best for coping with the heat. Shorts are acceptable in summer, although few Beijingers wear them. Warmer coats and gloves are necessary from November through to early April. A waterproof jacket and umbrella should be packed for changes in the weather, whatever the season. A sweater and light jacket are handy.

Temples and historic sites do not have clothing rules. Informal attire is acceptable nearly everywhere, including most fine restaurants. Formal wear (skirts, dresses, suits, ties) is seldom required, except for business travellers. Most hotels provide slippers but not bathrobes.

COMPLAINTS

Complaints may be made using the Beijing tourist hotline, Chinese language only (tel: 6513-0828). A quiet word to a guide, concierge or hotel desk about poor service can be productive; losing your temper usually solves nothing.

Complaints occasionally arise over excessive taxi charges. Many hotels now provide tourists with a card identifying each taxi as it is boarded. Use this card or copy down the taxi's number to file a complaint with your hotel reception. Complaints can also be directed to the Beijing Taxi Administration Bureau (tel: 6835-1150).

COMPUTERS AND THE INTERNET

Beijing has numerous internet cafés. While hotel business centres generally charge 2 or 3 yuan per minute for internet use, internet cafés charge between 10 and 20 yuan per hour. Many internet cafés are open from 7am until 2am; the best time to visit is during the day, when teenagers are at school. All are plastered with 'no smoking' signs, but these are routinely ignored – you can complain, but be prepared for a smoky environment. Many hotels and cafés (Starbucks and the small establishments on Nanluogu Xiang, for example) offer free wireless internet for customers.

Many hotel business centres also have personal computers and printers for hire, usually by the hour, with a full array of standard software available.

Check email	**Chá diànxìn**	查电信
Use the internet	**Shàng wǎng**	上网

CRIME AND SAFETY

Although Beijing remains a very safe city compared to most world capitals, petty street crime (particularly pickpocketing) is on the rise. Assaults and muggings of foreign visitors remain rare. The main office of the Public Security Bureau is at 9 Qianmen Dong Dajie, south of the Forbidden City. The emergency telephone number for the police is 110.

CUSTOMS AND ENTRY REQUIREMENTS

Foreign visitors are required to have a valid passport (good for at least six months after arrival date) and a visa issued by a Chinese embassy or consulate. The stamped visa is valid only for the dates specified.

Visas. A tourist visa is necessary for entering China and must be applied for in person or through an agent; mail-in applications are no longer accepted in the UK or US. If you need to extend your visa in

China, contact the Public Security Bureau, Visa Section, Andingmen Dongdajie (near the Lama Temple), tel: 8401-5294. The fine for overstaying a visa is a punitive 500 yuan per day.

On entry, a health declaration, entry card and customs declaration have to be completed. These forms are given out on the plane or at the airport on arrival. Note that no vaccinations or inoculations are currently required.

Customs. Those intending to stay less than six months in China can bring in duty free up to two bottles of alcohol and 400 cigarettes. Guns and 'dangerous' drugs are forbidden. Upon departure from China, Chinese antiques must contain a red wax seal for export.

Customs allowances when returning home are as follows. *Australia:* A\$900 of merchandise, 250 cigarettes or 250g of tobacco, 2.25 litres of alcohol. *Canada:* \$500 of merchandise, 200 cigarettes, 400 grams of tobacco, 50 cigars, 40 imperial ounces of alcohol. *UK:* £145 of merchandise, 200 cigarettes or 250g of tobacco or 50 cigars, 1 litre of spirits, 2 litres of wine. *New Zealand:* NZ\$700 of merchandise, 200 cigarettes or 250g of tobacco or 50 cigars, 1.125 litres of liquor or 4.5 litres of wine and beer. *US:* US\$800 of merchandise, 200 cigarettes, 100 cigars, 350g of tobacco, 1 litre of spirits, wine or beer.

Currency restrictions. Amounts of foreign currency equalling more than US\$10,000 must be declared on customs forms before entry, although there is no restriction on the amount brought into the country. Chinese currency (yuan) must be exchanged before departure at the Bank of China, since it is not convertible and may not be exchanged in your home country.

D

DRIVING

The Chinese drive on the right-hand side of the road. Rules, highways, traffic signals and road signs are similar to those in Western nations. So are Beijing's rush hours and traffic jams.

E

ELECTRICITY

The standard is 220-volt, 50-cycle AC. Hotels supply adapters, as the outlets come in a variety of configurations, the most common being the slanted 2-prong, the narrow round 2-pin and the 3-prong types. Bring your own set of modem adapters and transformers.

EMBASSIES

Australia	21 Dongzhimenwai Dajie; tel: 5140-4111
Canada	19 Dongzhimenwai Dajie; tel: 6532-3536
Ireland	3 Ritan Donglu; tel. 6532-2691
New Zealand	1 Dong'erjie, Ritan Lu; tel: 6532-2731
UK	11 Guanghua Lu; tel: 5192-4000
US	3 Xiushui Dongjie, Jianguomenwai; tel: 6532-3831

Embassy	**Dàshǐguǎn**	大使馆
Passport	**Hùzhào**	护照
Visa	**Qiānzhèng**	签证

EMERGENCIES

Police 110   **Fire** 119   **Ambulance** 120

If you don't speak Chinese, contact your hotel front desk.

G

GAY AND LESBIAN TRAVELLERS

There are local Chinese gay and lesbian support groups as well as a fair number of bars, clubs and saunas. Destination is a popular Western-style gay club on Workers' Stadium West Road, while West Wing is a lesbian bar in the ancient city gate of Deshengmen. Chinese are uncomfortable with public displays of affection, whatever the sexuality, so it's best to be discreet. The younger generation is very accepting of homosexuality and gay bashing is almost unheard of, although some older people find gays and lesbians perplexing.

GETTING THERE

By air. Beijing is served by over 30 international airlines, including its own Air China, which is usually the cheapest option. The trip is about 10 hours from the UK, 13 hours from the west coast of North America, 12 hours from Copenhagen, 13 hours from Australia and 18–20 hours from the east coast of North America.

Most airlines offer a choice of economy, business or first-class cabins. APEX fares are considerably lower than regular full fares, but they require advance purchase (14 days) and have other restrictions. Travel agents who use ticket consolidator services might be able to find even cheaper tickets (but often of the non-refundable variety). Bargain fares sometimes show up on internet travel sites. Many airlines code-share internationally, meaning you will start out on one nation's airline and transfer to another nation's to reach Beijing, all on the same single ticket. Flights are often heavily booked, so reserve as far ahead as possible.

By train. Beijing is connected to virtually all Chinese cities, including Hong Kong, via an extensive passenger rail system. There are also connections to Moscow via the Trans-Siberian Railway. Customs and immigration procedures are handled on board. China's most de-luxe train connects Hong Kong to Beijing, a 29-hour trip. The Beijing West Station, Asia's largest, and the old Beijing Railway Station both have special ticket counters and waiting rooms for foreigners. Train tickets can be purchased through hotel travel services, which add a nominal service charge.

| Airport | **Fēijīchǎng** | 飞机场 |
| Railway station | **Huǒchē zhàn** | 火车站 |

GUIDES AND TOURS

Because of language barriers, sharp cultural differences and the relative infancy of the Chinese travel industry, most visitors come to Beijing for the first time as part of a group. Travel agents can also set up customised trips for independent travellers who wish to book a hotel in advance and be met by a local English-speaking guide. Group tours are more expensive, but they are efficient and convenient.

If you are travelling independently, you can get your bearings in Beijing by signing up for a few of the day tours with English-speaking guides that are offered in all hotels. These tours provide a quick survey of Beijing's major sites. Taxis, the subway and bike hire are also inexpensive ways of touring the capital on your own.

For sites outside Beijing, such as the Great Wall, you can sign up for a day tour or hire a chauffeured car with an English-speaking guide at your hotel travel desk. Or you can take the slow, crowded, but interesting local and intercity buses to sites (as Beijingers do) or hire a taxi in the street for a day's touring (but negotiate the fare first).

China International Travel Service (CITS), with offices at 1 Dongdan (tel: 6522-6866; www.cits.com.cn), offers a wide range of group tours, creates customised itineraries and provides multilingual guides.

H

HEALTH AND MEDICAL CARE

Medications. It is easiest to bring your own prescription medicines with you, although there are hospitals that can give Western prescriptions. Colds, upset stomachs and diarrhoea are the most common ailments among travellers. Bring your own remedies, since pain relievers and other non-prescription medicines can be difficult to find.

Water. Do not drink water from the tap. The only water in Beijing that is safe to drink is bottled water (for sale everywhere) and the boiled water in hotel room flasks. Tap water is suitable for washing, but it is not safe for drinking.

Hospitals. Several hospitals and clinics provide international-calibre care for foreign residents and tourists. The Beijing United Family Health Centre (tel: 6433-3960), the Beijing AEA International Clinic and International SOS Clinic (tel: 6462-9100/12) all maintain 24-hour emergency facilities and pharmacies. Prices are similar to those in the West. Check if your health insurance covers you in China. If it does not, purchasing a short-term policy for overseas travel is recommended.

Pharmacy	**Yàodiàn**	药店
Hospital	**Yīyuàn**	医院
Doctor	**Dàifu/yīshēng**	大夫/医生

HOLIDAYS

National and local holidays observed in Beijing are listed below. Spring Festival (Chinese New Year) is the biggest holiday, lasting up to 15 days, concluding with the Lantern Festival. On the first three days, all banks, offices and many shops are closed. Banks, offices and many businesses close again for two days starting on 1 October, National Day, commemorating the founding of the People's Republic of China in 1949; large celebrations are staged at Tiananmen Square.

1 January	*New Year's Day*
January or February	*Spring Festival (Lunar New Year)*
January or February	*Lantern Festival*
	(15th day of first lunar month)
March or April	*Guanyin's Birthday*
	(50th day on lunar calendar)
April	*Qingming Festival (Festival of Light)*
1 May	*International Workers' Day*
June	*Dragon Boat Festival*
September or October	*Mid-Autumn Festival (Moon Festival)*
1 October	*National Day*

L

LANGUAGE

While every city and region of China has its own distinct dialect, Beijingers speak a version of Chinese that is the basis for the official spoken language of the nation (called *putonghua* or Mandarin Chinese). Nearly all Beijingers have taken classes in English (required by all schools), but outside of hotels and tourist spots, English is not well understood or commonly spoken.

Nevertheless, for ordinary shopping, dining and touring in the capital, it's not necessary to have Chinese language skills, as there are enough signs in English or *pinyin* (the official system for romanising Chinese words) to navigate by and enough clever vendors with whom to bargain. However, it would definitely be useful, particularly for independent travellers, to familiarise yourself a little with pronunciation. Even when asking the way to a place or for a street name, you need to know how it is pronounced correctly, otherwise you won't be understood.

Spoken Chinese is composed less of vowels and consonants than of syllables, consisting of a consonant of homonyms (words of different meaning but with identical spelling). In reality every syllable is pronounced with one of four tones (high, rising, falling-rising and falling). Tones make it difficult for foreigners to learn Chinese, since different tones give the same syllable a completely different meaning. An example of how tones affect meaning: *ma* pronounced with a high tone means 'mother', with a rising tone 'hemp', with a falling-rising tone 'horse', and with a falling tone 'to complain'. There are a standard set of diacritical marks to indicate which of the four tones is used:

mā = high and even tone
má = rising tone
mǎ = falling then rising tone
mà = falling tone

Pronouncing *pinyin* has its own nuances and complications. Among the biggest stumbling blocks are the following consonants (accompanied by approximate English equivalents):

c	like ts in the word 'i**ts**'
g	hard g as in '**g**ive'
h	like ch in Scottish 'lo**ch**'
j	like j in '**j**eer'
q	similar to ch in '**ch**eer'
x	like sh in '**sh**ip'
z	like ds in 'ki**ds**'
zh	like j in '**j**ug'

Some useful greetings:

Hello	**Nǐ hǎo**	你好
How are you?	**Nǐ hǎo ma?**	你好吗?
Thank you	**Xièxie**	谢谢
Goodbye	**Zài jiàn**	再见
My name is…	**Wǒ jiào…**	我叫…
All right	**Hǎo**	好
Not all right	**Bù hǎo**	不好
Can you speak English?	**Nín huì shuō Yīngyǔ ma?**	您会说英语吗?
I do not understand	**Wǒ bù dǒng**	我不懂
Do you understand?	**Nín dǒng ma?**	您懂吗?
Please speak a little more slowly	**Qǐng nín shuō màn yìdiǎnr**	请您说慢一点儿
Please	**Qǐng**	请/谢谢
Sorry	**Duìbùqǐ**	对不起

The Berlitz *Mandarin Chinese Phrase Book & Dictionary* covers most of the situations you are likely to encounter in China.

LAUNDRY AND DRY CLEANING

Most hotels offer excellent same-day or next-day laundry and dry-cleaning services at reasonable prices. Self-service laundrettes are rare, and laundrettes outside of hotels are inconvenient for tourists to use.

M

MAPS

City maps are for sale in hotel gift shops and from street-corner vendors. The most useful maps label streets and sites in Chinese script, *pinyin* (romanised Chinese) and English or other Western languages. Beijing maps can be purchased in advance from bookstores abroad.

MEDIA

Newspapers and magazines. China's official English-language newspaper, *China Daily,* is available free at hotel desks from Monday to Saturday. It includes world news, Chinese news and entertainment listings for Beijing. Free monthly Beijing newspapers in English, focusing on tourist sites and entertainment, are also distributed to many hotels and cafés. Foreign magazines and newspapers – including *International Herald Tribune, USA Today,* Hong Kong's *South China Morning Post,* and Asian editions of the *Wall Street Journal, Time* and *Newsweek* – can be purchased at kiosks and gift shops in major luxury hotels. For local listings, pick up a copy of the what's-on magazine *That's Beijing.*

Television. Most major hotels carry via satellite two channels of Chinese Central Television (CCTV) and three channels of Beijing Television (BTV), all in the Chinese language. Other common selections include Star TV (Hong Kong-based, with one English-language station), CNN, CNBC, BBC, ESPN, MTV and NHK (Japanese language). The five-star hotels offer a wider selection, including other stations from Europe and Australia. In-room movie services usually include pay per view films or HBO.

MONEY

Currency. China's currency, called *renminbi* ('the people's money') and often abbreviated as 'RMB', is also called the *yuan* or the *kuai*. The yuan is divided into 100 *fen*. Ten fen equal one *jiao* (also called *mao*). For most transactions, you will use yuan notes in denominations of 1, 5, 10, 20, 50 and 100.

Currency exchange. Foreign currency and travellers' cheques can be exchanged for yuan at the Bank of China and hotel exchange counters. Beijing Capital International Airport maintains a branch of the Bank of China specialising in currency exchange. The exchange rates at each outlet vary only slightly; you will receive a better exchange rate for travellers' cheques than for cash. A passport is required for all currency transactions. The airport also has fast and convenient automated currency-exchange machines. The yuan was revalued in 2005, allowing greater exchange rate flexibility.

Credit cards. Major credit cards can be used in most large shops and restaurants. Look for the familiar emblems (Visa, MasterCard, American Express, Diner's Club, JCB). The Eurocard is accepted at very few locations. Major hotels accept credit cards for payment of all bills, including hotel restaurants. Some branches of the Bank of China and some hotels can also make cash advances on credit cards, but charge a 4 percent commission.

Cash machines/ATMs. Many ATMs now accept international cards. Look out for machines that feature Visa, American Express and other international credit-card logos. Larger branches at the Bank of China (at Wangfujing, Jianguomen and elsewhere) are the most reliable. Before visiting, ask your credit-card company or bank for a list of cash machines in Beijing.

Travellers' cheque	**Lǚxíng zhīpiào**	旅行支票
Credit card	**Xìnyòngkǎ**	信用卡
Foreign currency	**Wàihuìquàn**	外汇券

Cash. China is still a cash society and Beijing is no exception. Most transactions outside large hotels, restaurants and shops catering largely to Westerners require payment in yuan.

How much?	**Duōshǎo?**	多少
Too expensive, thank you	**Tài guì le, xièxie**	这个多少钱？ 太贵了，谢谢
Very expensive	**Hěn guì**	很贵
A little (bit)	**Yìdiǎnr**	一点儿
A lot	**Duō**	多

O

OPENING HOURS

State-owned restaurants and shops close at around 8.30 or 9pm, but private establishments stay open much later. Chain grocery stores normally open around 8am or 9am and close at 9pm. Major shopping malls stay open until 10pm or later, with shops inside closing at different times – clothing shops are the first to close. All stores are open daily, including weekends, and many of them open on national holidays.

P

POLICE

Beijing police are usually courteous and helpful. Their main office (the Public Security Bureau) is at 85 Beichizi Lu, on the east side of the Forbidden City. The police emergency phone number is 110.

POST OFFICES

The main International Post Office, on the Second Ring Road East (Jianguomen Beidajie), is open every day 8am–6pm (tel: 6512-

8120). Hotels often sell postage stamps and will post items for you. Letters and postcards to and from China take about six days.

Air mail	**Hángkōng xìn**	航空信
Postage stamp	**Yóupiào**	邮票
Post Office	**Yóujú**	邮局

PUBLIC TRANSPORT

The subway is the fastest form of public transport in Beijing. City buses are the cheapest but also the most crowded, slow and difficult way to get around. Taxis are plentiful and relatively cheap. Bicycles are sometimes the fastest way to get through the busy streets.

Subway. All journeys costs 2 yuan (US$0.35). Several new lines will open before the Olympics, but as of March 2008, there are four main lines (operating 6am–11pm). Line 1 (red), the crosstown line, runs along Chang'an Avenue, while Line 2 (blue), the circle line, traces the route of the Second Ring Road, Line 10 (dark blue) runs north–south past the Lama Temple to the Temple of Heaven, and Line 13 (yellow) is a slow overground link that skirts Haidian district and the north.

Tickets are sold at booths one level above the train platforms. Subway maps (in Chinese and in romanised *pinyin* letters) are posted inside the train car. A recording announces in Chinese and in English each upcoming stop. The carriages are clean and seldom crowded.

Buses. Although the buses are very cheap (most rides cost just 1 yuan), they are bewildering to use. Arm yourself with a city map labelled in Chinese. A roving conductor collects fares after you board. The red-and-white buses service every city centre bus stop, with Nos 103 and 104 running the length of Chang'an Avenue. Keep an eye on your belongings as thieves operate on the buses.

Taxis. Cheap and convenient. Taxis, generally two-coloured Citroens (yellow and green, or yellow and blue), have a minimum fare of 10 yuan and cost 2 yuan per km after the initial 3km. Between

11pm and 5am, the fares increase. All taxis are metered but sometimes a driver may try to quote a flat rate. Do not accept this if you are just going one way, as it won't be cheaper than the meter charge. **Bicycles** *(see also page 109).* If you want to experience travelling through the city at a cyclist's pace but don't feel like cycling yourself, pedicabs (or trishaws) can be hired near many tourist sites.

Bus	**Gōnggòng qìchē**	公共汽车
Taxi	**Chūzū qìchē**	出租汽车
Bicycle	**Zìxíngchē**	自行车

R

RELIGION

Fewer than 10 percent of Beijingers are affiliated with any religious organisation, although Daoism, Buddhism and Christianity are gaining many new adherents. Beijing also has over 200,000 Muslims.

Beijing's main Catholic congregation worships at the South Cathedral (Nan Tang). There are Protestant congregations and churches as well. Check with your hotel about service times and locations.

T

TELEPHONE

The international country code for China is 86. The city code for Beijing is 10.

Calling from abroad. To place a long-distance call to Beijing from overseas, dial the international access code used in your country, then 86, then 10, then the 8-digit Beijing phone number.

Calling from inside China. *Domestic calls:* To call Beijing from other destinations in China, you must add a zero to the city code: 0+10. To call from Beijing to another city in China, dial 0, then that city's code and the local number. *International calls:* To reach an overseas destination, dial China's international access code, 00, then the country code, then the area/city code minus the initial zero, and then the local phone number. The country code for the US and Canada is 1, for the UK 44, for Australia 61, for New Zealand 64, for Ireland 353 and for South Africa 27. Dial 115 for an international operator in Beijing.

International calls from hotels are expensive. In top hotels, you can use credit cards and international phone cards. China's rates are higher than those of most Western countries; costs are halved after 6pm and at weekends. For cheaper overseas call rates, buy IDD cards from magazine kiosks in the street. You first dial the number on the card, type a serial number and a pin number written on the card – instructions are in English – and then dial the number you want. A 100 yuan denominated card costs about 35 to 40 yuan to buy and gives you about 20–30 minutes of call time if you're dialing the US or the UK.

Phone booths (requiring local phone cards, which can be purchased in hotels and shops) can be found on many major city-centre streets. Some are equipped to handle long-distance and international calls.

Most GSM mobiles will work fine in China; either contact your service provider about roaming (expensive) or buy a SIM card at the airport when you arrive for 100 yuan. China Mobile gives the best coverage and you can buy 100 yuan top-up cards at magazine kiosks.

Telephone	**Diànhuà**	电话
Long-distance call	**Chángtú diànhuà**	长途电话
International call	**Guójì diànhuà**	国际电话

TICKETS

It is best to book tickets for entertainment and events – such as the opera or acrobatics – through hotel travel desks or the hotel concierge, rather than at the venue's crowded and often distant ticket office.

TIME ZONES

Although China stretches across four time zones, all of China set their clocks to Beijing time. Beijing is eight hours ahead of Greenwich Mean Time (GMT+8). It is 13 hours ahead of New York, 16 hours ahead of Los Angeles and two hours behind Australia.

The following chart lists the times in selected cities in winter months when it is 8pm in Beijing. China does not employ Daylight Saving Time in the summer, when times in many parts of the world are an hour later.

Los Angeles	New York	London	**Beijing**	Sydney	Auckland
4am	7am	noon	**8pm**	10pm	midnight

TIPPING

Tipping is not customary in China. However, in current practice porters, room-service staff, waiters in large hotels and restaurants and hired guides are usually tipped 10–20 yuan, and taxi drivers appreciate finding their fares have been overpaid by a few yuan.

TOILETS

All public toilets are free and their standards are much higher than in the past. The city government has allocated 100 million yuan per year for further upgrading in the run-up to the Olympics. But many are best avoided except in dire need (it is advisable to carry tissues, as they do not have paper). The best option is to go to a hotel or restaurant.

Toilet	**Cèsuǒ**	厕所

TOURIST INFORMATION

Beijing's tourist information offices are not especially helpful and mainly exist to sell tours. Your best sources of tourist information are your hotel tour desk or concierge and the free local monthly papers in English *(see page 120)*.

Before your trip. Overseas, the state-run China International Travel Service (CITS; www.cits.com.cn) has opened several China National Tourist Offices (CNTO) to provide tourist information:

Los Angeles area   550 North Brand Boulevard, Suite 910, Glendale, CA 91203; tel: 1-800 670 2228

London   4 Glentworth St, London NW1; tel: 020 7935 9787

New York City   350 5th Avenue, Suite 6413, New York, NY 10118; tel: 1-888 760 8218

Sydney   11th Floor, 234 George Street, Sydney, New South Wales, 2000, Australia; tel: (612) 9252 9838

Toronto   80 University Avenue, Suite 806, Toronto, ON M5G 1V2; tel: (416) 599 6636

WEBSITES

Some useful websites for Beijing include:
• **www.beijinghighlights.com** Beijing tour planning.
• **www.bjta.gov.cn** Municipal website – features travel news and tips, and information on shopping and restaurants.
• **www.btmbeijing.com** *Beijing This Month* – features events calendar, city map, useful advertisements and links for hotel reservations.
• **www.cbw.com** Business, trade and travel information.
• **www.thebeijinger.com** Online listings.
• **www.tour-beijing.com** Tour operator based in Beijing.

WEIGHTS AND MEASURES

China uses the metric system, although traditional measurements endure in the marketplace.

Recommended Hotels

Most travellers prefer four- and five-star hotels (as rated by the government), as these have clean, modern facilities and English-speaking staff. Some of the top five-star hotels are affiliated with major hotel chains and have international management teams. Full Western breakfast buffets are not routinely included in room rates, nor is transport to the airport, so enquire ahead about both.

Reservations well in advance are strongly recommended from May through to October. Many Beijing hotels are completely booked in May and October. To phone a hotel from abroad, be sure to dial China's country code (86) and Beijing's city code (10) before the eight-digit local number.

Major hotels (three-star and above) add a 15 percent service charge and levy a small city development tax (neither reflected in the prices listed below). Nearly all of these hotels accept international credit cards (although few Beijing hotels accept the Eurocard).

As a basic guide, we have used the symbols below to indicate average prices, per night, for a double room with bath. (Note that the symbols are not necessarily equivalent to the star ratings provided by the Chinese Government.)

$$$$$	over 2,000 yuan
$$$$	1,500–2,000 yuan
$$$	1,000–1,500 yuan
$$	500–1,000 yuan
$	below 500 yuan

CENTRAL DISTRICT (DONGCHENG)

Beijing Hotel (Beijing Fandian) **$$$$** *35 Dongchang'an Jie, tel: 6513-7766, fax: 6523-2395.* Original section of Beijing's historic hotel opened in 1917. The west wing was added in 1954 and the east wing, on Wangfujing Dajie, was added in 1974. Extensive remodelling and modernisation have left only a few reminders of Old Peking, but the ballroom and long lobby have touches of pre-revolutionary days. 1,432 rooms.

Beijing International Hotel (Beijing Guoji Fandian) **$$$$** *9 Jian-guomenwai Dajie, tel: 6512-6688, fax: 6512-9972, www.bih.com.cn.* A short walk east of the Forbidden City, this 29-storey Chinese-managed hotel has over 12 restaurants and a bowling alley. Rooms are large and well-appointed, but housekeeping is a problem. 1,002 rooms.

Grand Hotel Beijing (Guibinluo Fandian) **$$$$$** *35 Dongchang'an Jie, tel: 6513-7788, fax: 6513-0050, www.grandhotelbeijing.com.* The west wing of the historic Beijing Hotel, this de-luxe modern addition with seven-storey marble atrium is the closest hotel to the Forbidden City. Its elegant rooms, with separate baths and showers, are large and feature a full range of amenities. 218 rooms.

Grand Hyatt Beijing (Dongfang Junyne Da Jindian) **$$$$$** *1 Dongchang'an Jie, tel: 8518-1234, fax: 8518-0000, www.beijing.grand.hyatt.com.* Situated in the Oriental Plaza, this hotel is ideally situated for Wangfujing Street, Tiananmen Square and the Forbidden City. One of Bejing's top hotels. The lobby is particularly impressive at night as it curls around a glowing fountain. 695 rooms.

Haoyuan Hotel $$ *Shijia Hutong, Dongsinan Dajie, tel: 6512-5557, fax: 6525-3179, www.haoyuanhotel.com.* Hidden away in a narrow alley close to The Peninsula Beijing, the Haoyuan's rooms surround two quiet courtyards. The buildings are a traditional combination of brick and red-lacquered wood, with curved tiles on the roofs. A small restaurant serves hearty traditional fare. Book well in advance. 19 rooms.

Holiday Inn Crowne Plaza (Guoji Yiyuan Huangguan Jiari Fandian) **$$$** *48 Wangfujing Dajie, tel: 5911-9999, fax: 5911-9998, www.holiday-inn.com.* Art is the theme of this five-star boutique hotel (with its own contemporary Chinese art gallery), located on Beijing's top shopping street close to the Forbidden City. Rooms in the Crowne Plaza face either the street or the nine-storey atrium, where traditional Chinese music is performed in the evenings. 720 rooms.

Hotel Côté Cour SL $$$ *70 Yanyue Hutong, tel: 6512-8020, fax: 6512-7295, www.hotelcotecoursl.com.* This designer hotel is set around a beautiful courtyard complete with lily pond. Rooms are furnished in silks and wood. Breakfast in the funky dining room is included in the price. 14 rooms.

Hotel Kapok (Beijing Huajing Mumian Hua Jiudian) **$$$** *16 Donghuamen Dajie, tel: 6525-9988, fax: 6528-9512, www.hotelkapok. com.* One of Beijing's first boutique hotels, the Kapok glows green from the outside and is an attractive mix of glass and bamboo inside. Rooms are a little dinky but the bathrooms are equipped with power showers. The Forbidden City is a short walk to the west. 89 rooms.

The Peninsula Beijing (Wangfu Fandian) **$$$$$** *8 Jingyu Hutong, Wangfujing Dajie, tel: 8516-2888, fax: 6510-6311, www.beijing. peninsula.com.* Beijing centre's grand hotel, with a fleet of Rolls-Royces at the door and a waterfall in the lobby. The Peninsula contains two floors of high-priced international shops and superb restaurants. Rooms are spacious, with every amenity imaginable, including bathrobes and safe drinking-water dispensers. 530 rooms.

Raffles Beijing Hotel (Beijing Fandian Laifoshi) **$$$$$** *33 Chang'an Dongdajie, tel: 6526-3388, fax: 8500-4380, http://beijing.raffles.com.* The most elegant of the three hotels in the Beijing Hotel complex on Chang'an Jie. This place oozes colonial elegance. 171 rooms.

EASTERN DISTRICT (CHAOYANG)

China World Hotel (Zhongguo Da Fandian) **$$$$$** *1 Jianguomenwai Dajie, tel: 6505-2266, fax: 6505-0828, www.shangri-la.com.* Widely regarded as one of Beijing's best hotels (a favourite of diplomatic and corporate officials), this Shangri-La hotel is located on the eastern extension of Chang'an Avenue next to a subway station on the Third Ring Road. The business centre is Beijing's best. The hotel is inside the China World Trade Centre, a shopping and office plaza. Rooms are large, elegant and well-maintained. 716 rooms.

Jianguo Hotel (Jianguo Fandian) **$$$$** *5 Jianguomenwai Dajie, tel: 6500-2233, fax: 6500-2871.* China's first joint-venture hotel (1982), renovated in 2007. Great-value rooms with four-star comfort at a fraction of the price you'd pay at an international chain. It has a huge pool. Convenient for the Friendship Store. 460 rooms.

Kerry Centre Hotel (Beijing Jiali Zhongxin Fandian) **$$$$$** *1 Guanghua Lu, tel: 6561-8833, fax: 6561-2626, www.shangri-la. com.* This hotel has highly efficient service and de-luxe facilities, headlined by a roof garden with jogging track, in-line skating and a children's play area. The rooms are in high-tech style, featuring broadband internet access and movie channels. 487 rooms.

St Regis Hotel $$$$$ *21 Jianguomenwai Dajie, tel: 6460-6688, fax: 6460-3299, www.stregis.com.* This luxurious hotel enjoys a prime Chaoyang location. The hotel's Press Club Bar is popular with the foreign business community. 273 rooms.

Swissôtel Beijing (Beijing Gang Ao Zhongxin) **$$$$$** *Hong Kong Macau Centre, 2 Chaoyangmen Beidajie, tel: 6553-2288, fax: 6501-2501, www.beijing.swissotel.com.* Presided over by the Swissair Swissôtel, this five-star hotel has a European feel, well-maintained rooms and excellent facilities, including a medical clinic. The fourth floor is barrier-free for travellers with disabilities. 430 rooms.

Traders Hotel (Gumao Fandian) **$$$$** *1 Jianguomenwai Dajie, tel: 6505-2277, fax: 6505-0838, www.shangri-la.com.* Perhaps Beijing's best four-star hotel, with good service, food and accommodation, Traders (managed by Shangri-La) has close links to the five-star China World Hotel next door, which is more expensive. Its underground shopping centre includes an indoor ice-skating rink. Rooms are comfortable and spacious, the marble bathrooms are luxurious and the large hotel business centre has an excellent bookshop. 570 rooms.

NORTHEAST DISTRICT (CHAOYANG)

Beijing Hilton Hotel (Xierdun Fandian) **$$$$$** *1 Dongfang Lu, Dongsanhuan Beilu, tel: 5865-5000, fax: 5865-5800, www.beijing. hilton.com.* The Hilton is a fine international hotel, popular with Western business travellers. Services and maintenance are first-rate. 340 rooms.

Great Wall Sheraton (Changcheng Fandian) **$$$$$** *10 Dong-sanhuan Beilu, tel: 6590-5566, fax: 6590-5398, www.sheraton.com/beijing.* The first internationally managed five-star hotel to open (1984) on the Third Ring Road North, the Great Wall sets a high standard with its services and many facilities. The spacious rooms feature internet access and compact marble bathrooms. 850 rooms.

Holiday Inn Lido (Lidu Jiari Fandian) **$$$** *Jichang Lu, Jiangtai Lu, tel: 6437-6688, fax: 6437-6237, www.beijing-lido.holiday-inn.com.* Located halfway between city centre and the airport (16km/ 10 miles), this hotel is a place unto itself. The facilities, including a bank, a bowling alley and a Western supermarket and chemist, are unequalled in China. The rooms are more basic but come with king-sized beds, satellite TV and clean modern bathrooms. Just 20 minutes from the airport. 430 rooms.

Kempinski Hotel (Kaibinsiji Fandian) **$$$$$** *50 Liangmaqiao Lu, Lufthansa Centre, tel: 6465-3388, fax: 6465-1202, www.kempinski-beijing.com.* With impeccable service and upkeep under German management, the Kempinski is popular with Europeans. The hotel has a deli and a German pub, and it is attached to the Friendship Shopping City at the Lufthansa Centre. Rooms are large, there's a fitness centre, and a shuttle bus serves both the airport and downtown. 526 rooms.

Radisson SAS Royal Hotel (Huangjia Da Fandian) **$$$$$** *6a Beisanhuan Donglu, tel: 6466-3388, fax: 6465-3181, www.radisson.com.* The most stylish rooms in the capital come in three kinds of décor: Oriental, High-Tech and Art Deco. All rooms are large and well maintained. The service is excellent, facilities extensive, and the atmosphere European. This is the best four-star hotel in northeast Beijing (as well as the priciest in its class). 362 rooms.

Sino-Swiss Hotel Beijing Airport **$$$$** *Xiao Tianzhu Village, Capital Airport, Shunyi County, tel: 6456-5588, fax: 6456-1234, www.sino-swisshotel.com.* Situated beyond the urban smog belt, this is Beijing's only de-luxe airport hotel (15 minutes on the free shuttle) – and its only resort hotel. Rooms are large and the atmosphere is European. Resort facilities include the capital's only

natural thermal hot springs pool, interconnected indoor and outdoor swimming pools and a beach-sand volleyball court. 400 rooms.

NORTHWEST DISTRICTS (XICHENG, HAIDIAN)

Crowne Plaza Wuzhou (Wuzhou Huanguan Jiari Jiudian) **$$$$** *8
Beisihuan Zhonglu, Chaoyang,* tel: 8498-2288, fax: 8499-2933. A
business hotel a 10-minute walk from the Olympic Village. If you're
a not a business traveller or an Olympic tourist, however, it's a bit
bleak and isolated. 478 rooms.

Holiday Inn Downtown (Jindu Jiari Fandian) **$$$** *98 Beilishi Lu,* tel:
6833-8822, fax: 6834-0696, *www.holidayinn.com.* Not exactly
downtown, but just a block from the Fuchengmen subway station
and Vantone shopping plaza, this Holiday Inn is highly efficient and
comfortable: a good deal for the price. 328 rooms.

InterContinental Beijing Financial Street (Zhouji Jiudian) **$$$$–
$$$$$** *11 Financial Street,* tel: 5852-5888, fax: 5852-5999, *www.
intercontinental.com/icbeijing.* Providing five-star luxury and im-
peccable service, the InterContinental sports a magnificent atrium
but is a bit like a commercial building on first impressions. Rooms
are spacious, modern and luxuriously appointed. 330 rooms.

Shangri-La Beijing Hotel (Xiangge Lila Fandian) **$$$$$** *29
Zizhuyuan Lu,* tel: 6841-2211, fax: 6841-8002, *www.shangri-la.
com.* One of the top hotels in China, the Shangri-La has set high
standards for service and elegance since it opened in 1986. The clas-
sic Chinese garden is a focal point and symbol of its serene atmos-
phere, far from the jarring energy of the city centre. The rooms are
among Beijing's largest and best appointed. 650 rooms.

Westin Beijing Financial Street (Beijing Jinrongjie Weisiting Da
Jiudian) **$$$$–$$$$$** *98 Financial Street,* tel: 6606-8866, *http://
westin.com/beijingfinancial.* This five-star hotel has generated most-
ly rave reviews. Luxuries include mega-spray showers and their sig-
nature 'heavenly beds'. Other highlights include a fabulous Sunday
brunch and an infinity pool with underwater music. 486 rooms.

Commune by the Great Wall (Changcheng Jiaoxia de Gongshe Kaibinsiji Fandian) **$$$$$** *Shuiguan Great Wall Exit, Badaling Highway, tel: 5878-8205, fax: 6567-8383, www.communebythegreatwall.com.* This is a unique village of architect-designed houses on a hillside capped by the Great Wall. The designs range in style from funky bamboo structures to strange, carpark-like concrete blocks. Guests rent a room in a house of about six bedrooms, so you share a kitchen and huge lounge with other guests. There is private access to the wall and a feeling of open space – the houses have cathedral-high ceilings and lots of glass is employed to maximise this effect – but you need to be fit, as the houses are a good walk from the main building, which contains the restaurants and lobby. Service ranges from great to indifferent. 236 rooms.

Qianmen Jianguo Hotel $$$ *175 Yongan Lu, tel: 6301-6688, fax: 6301-3883, www.qianmenhotel.com.* Comfortable hotel in the south of the city between the Temple of Heaven and Niu Jie Mosque, the Qianmen stages nightly Beijing Opera performances. 403 rooms.

CHENGDE

Puning Hotel $ *Puning Lu, West Yard of Puning Temple, tel: (0314) 205-8888, fax: (0314) 205-8998.* Belonging to the Puning temple, this newly built, traditional-style hotel has an excellent vegetarian restaurant. The plumbing is not perfect but the serenity of the location and early-morning chanting of the lamas make up for its shortcomings. 100 rooms.

GREAT WALL

Red Capital Ranch $$$$ *28 Xiaguandi Village, Yanxi Township, Huairou, tel: 8401-8886, www.redcapitalclub.com.cn.* A Manchurian hunting lodge set in the shadow of the Great Wall. Each room is a luxuriously restored villa. Fine restaurant and spa.

Recommended Restaurants

Beijing has a fabulous and diverse dining scene. Visitors can enjoy the full range of Chinese cuisine from cheap snacks to upmarket restaurants, as well as a cosmopolitan spread of the world's food from Mexican to Russian to Ethiopian. Many top restaurants can be found in five-star hotels, but there are also scores of private establishments that are top notch. Finally, for the less adventurous there are familiar fast-food outlets such as McDonald's and KFC.

Most restaurants, including many in hotels, keep traditional Chinese hours, which are typically 7–9am for breakfast, 11.30am–2pm for lunch and 5.30–9pm for dinner. Some hotels have 24-hour lobby restaurants. Chopsticks are the rule at Chinese restaurants, although you will often be given a knife and fork if you ask.

Beijingers spend more on food than on housing, but restaurant prices here are lower than in most Western capitals. Reservations are recommended in the more expensive establishments, particularly at weekends. Tipping is not necessary in private restaurants, but a small gratuity is acceptable; most hotel outlets include a 15 percent service charge. The following symbols indicate the cost of an average dinner, per person, excluding drinks:

$$$$	above 500 yuan
$$$	200–500 yuan
$$	100–200 yuan
$	below 100 yuan

CENTRAL DISTRICT (DONGCHENG)

The CourtYard $$$$ *95 Donghuamen Dajie, tel: 6526-8883, www.courtyard-gallery.com*. This upscale contemporary bistro, located on the moat of the Forbidden City, is among the city's most popular spots. The East-West fusion dishes blend Chinese and fresh Western ingredients in everything from salads to blackened salmon. A gallery features contemporary Chinese artists, and there's a cigar divan for a relaxing drink. Open daily 6–10pm.

Made in China $$$$ *Grand Hyatt Hotel, Oriental Plaza, tel: 6510-9608*. Often voted the best place to have Beijing duck. The restaurant has situated the kitchen in the dining room, and chefs work behind glass screens, so that you eat to the sound of sizzling woks. Open daily 7–10am, 11.30am–2.30pm and 5.30–10pm.

Red Capital Club (Xin Hongzi Julebu) **$$$$** *66 Dongsijiu Tiao, Dongcheng, tel: 8401-6152*. Red Capital Club is situated in a lovingly restored courtyard house. The décor here evokes 1950s China, and much of the furniture was once used by high-level leaders. The menu features the favourite dishes of such leaders as Mao Zedong and Deng Xiaoping. Open daily 6pm–1am.

EASTERN DISTRICT (CHAOYANG)

Aria $$$ *China World Hotel, Levels 2–3, 1 Jianguomenwai Dajie, tel: 6505-2266, ext. 36*. Jazz is the focus at this stylish grill where there is a piano, open kitchen, well-stocked wine bar and a menu of excellent American and Continental dishes. The entrées range from rotisserie-grilled fish to imported steaks and pastas. Open daily 11.30am–midnight.

Dongbeiren $–$$ *A1 Xinzhong Jie, Dongzhimenwai, tel: 6415-2855*. Dongeiren is a jolly Manchurian Dumpling House, where the dumplings come in coloured dough, and the wait staff wear country print and sing their way through dinner. Great cheap, hearty food from the north. Open daily 11am–10pm.

Haitanghua Pyongyang $$–$$$ *8 Xinyuanxili Zongjie, tel: 6461-6295*. This North Korean restaurant is a bit like a time capsule of the bad old days of 1950s communism. All the waitresses, very pretty and very friendly, hail from the hermit kingdom. The food is comparatively expensive and, while perfectly good, is not as tasty as some of the South Korean restaurants in town. But it's worth eating here to catch a glimpse of another world and to watch the North Korean spooks with their slicked-back hair slip in and out of their private dining rooms. Open daily 11am–2.30pm, 5–10.30pm.

Justine's $$$$ *Jianguo Hotel, 5 Jianguomenwai Dajie, tel: 6500-2233, ext. 8039.* French cooking and a touch of European elegance, complete with chandeliers and crystal, have made Justine's a favourite with romantics. Normandy shellfish dishes, fresh oysters, goose liver and the rack of lamb headline the menu. Open daily 6.30am–9.30am, noon–2.30pm and 6pm–10.30pm.

Makye Ame $$ *A11 Xiushui Nanjie, Jianguomenwai Dajie, tel: 6506-9616.* An intimate restaurant with Tibetan art and furnishings and Tibetan-style dishes. Nightly floor show is exhilarating, especially when you're called upon to get involved. Open daily 11.30–2am.

Pete's Tex Mex $–$$ *88A St Regis, 21 Jianguomen Waidajie, tel: 8532-2449.* This family-friendly place serves big, chunky meals, heavy on the beans and cheese. The décor is a little 'Mexican kindergarten', but its kitsch glory matches the friendly yet goofy service. Open daily 7.30am–11.30pm.

Purple Haze $$–$$$ *Unnamed hutong opposite Workers' Stadium North Gate, Gongti Bei Lu, tel: 6413-0899.* Live jazz and the colourful soft furnishings give this establishment a laid-back feel. While the atmosphere is warm and muffled, the food is rich and tasty – creamy coconut curries, rich blackcurrant cheesecakes and spicy seafood – and there's free internet access. It's not too expensive either. Open daily 11am–11pm.

Salt $$$ *9 Jiangtai Xilu (opposite the Japanese School), Lido, tel: 6437-8457.* One of Beijing's newest and hottest new restaurants, Salt serves international food in an open kitchen lounge. Prices are a bit on the steep side, but most people rate the set menus as value for money. Don't expect massive helpings of food, but the flavours win over most customers. A particular favourite is the warm chocolate soufflé cake with molten white chocolate centre. Reservations essential. Open Tue–Sat noon–3pm and 6–10.30pm.

South Beauty $$–$$$ *4/F Oriental Kenzo Square, 21 Dongzhimenwai Zongjie (also branches in Oriental Plaza, Pacific Century Place and China World), tel: 8447-6171.* Lovely Sichuan food is served up by this restaurant chain. The décor combines traditional Chinese elements, such as opera masks, with modern design. Some of the dishes are cooked at the table with hot stones and other props. The food can be as spicy as you wish.

Summer Palace $$$ *China World Hotel, Level 2, 1 Jianguomenwai Dajie, tel: 6505-2266, ext. 34.* With cuisine, service and décor consistently impeccable, this might be the best Cantonese restaurant in Beijing and not a bad place to try the capital's own speciality, Beijing duck. The atmosphere is upscale but informal, the waiters skilled but not pushy. Open daily 11.30am–2pm and 6–10pm.

Xihe Yaju $$ *Northeast gate, Ritan Park, Ritan Dong Lu, tel: 8561-7643.* Situated in an old Qing Dynasty courtyard mansion, this is a fine place to try reasonably priced Sichuan and Cantonese dishes, with patio seating in the summer. The chicken with peanuts *(gong bao jiding)* is inexpensive and not too spicy. The same can be said of the steamed grass carp. Open daily 11am–2pm and 5pm–10pm. No credit cards.

NORTHERN AND BACK LAKES DISTRICTS

Ba Guo Bu Yi $$ *89-3 Dianmen Dongdajie, tel: 6400-8888.* Ba Guo Bu Yi delights the tourists with its wicked *bian lian* ('face-changing shows') from Sichuan Opera. The kitchen serves authentic Sichuan dishes that can be toned down on request. Open daily 10am–2pm, 5–9.30pm.

Beijing Noodle King (Jingweimian Dawang) **$** *35 Dianmen Xidajie, Xicheng District, tel: 6405-6666.* A bustling, bright place with a sedan chair outside and doormen in old-style clothing and fake braids who shout out the arrival of each guest. Open daily 10.30am–10.30pm.

Fangshan Restaurant $$$$ *1 Wenjin Jie, inside Beihai Park south gate, tel: 6401-1889.* Beijing's first and oldest imperial restaurant is a courtyard mansion on the north shore of a former royal pleasure park. Imperial Beijing cuisine consists of hearty, simple fare: steamed pastries, stir-fried peas, roast duck and chicken, and beancurd cakes. But you'll also find expensive delicacies such as poached lake trout *(tian xiang bao yu)*. The décor is straight out of Old China. Open daily 11am–1.30pm and 5–8pm.

Hutong Pizza $$ *9 Yindingqiao Hutong, Houhai; tel: 6617-5916*. This pizzeria has been around for a while and is always buzzing. It's famous for its massive, crispy square-shaped pizzas but the rest of the menu, such as burgers (including beanburgers), chips and lasagne, are pretty good too. Open daily noon–11pm

Kaorouji $$ *14 Qianhai Dongyan, tel: 6404-2554*. This is an old Muslim restaurant popular with Beijing's Hui residents. The caged mynah birds that greet diners in Chinese as they enter the restaurant are always a hit with children. Staff may also be able to arrange for a meal to be eaten on a boat on nearby Qianhai Lake. Open daily 11am–2pm and 5–11pm.

Kongyiji $$ *Shichahai Houhai Nanan, tel: 6618-4917*. This popular themed diner recreates the ancient flavours of Shaoxing, the southern home town of famed writer Lu Xun. Reservations advised. Open daily 11am–10pm.

Lao Han Zi $–$$ *Shichahai Qianhai Nan Yan, tel: 6404-2259*. A sprawling restaurant with a lantern-hung patio that specialises in the wholesome food of the Hakka people. Lao Han Zi is very popular – testament to the great food – but the service is spotty as a result. Try the perch in tinfoil – it's their speciality. Open daily 11am–10.30pm.

Mei Mansion $$$$ *24 Da Xiang Feng Hutong, tel: 6612-6845*. This pleasant restaurant features food created for the great Beijing Opera star, Mei Lanfang. Mei was a northerner but his chef was a southerner who created a kind of north-south fusion cuisine which the family reportedly still eats to this day. Open daily 11am–2pm and 5.30–9pm.

Mirch Masala $–$$ *60-2 Nanluogu Xiang, tel: 6406-4347*. Without doubt this Indian establishment is Nanluogu Xiang's best restaurant. This is a cosy, friendly place, and the food is fresh and tasty.

There's draught beer, good, inexpensive wines and some interesting Hindu kitsch. Open daily 11am–2.30pm, 5–10.30pm.

Passby Bar $–$$ *108 Nanluogu Xiang, tel: 8403-8004.* Passby was one of the first on this *hutong* and it still has a massive following. While it has the feel of a traveller's café – lots of books and travel photos – it's remarkably popular with local Chinese. It's a nice courtyard place, the food is mildly good Italian – pastas and pizza – and they do a mean draught beer. Open daily 9.30am–2pm, 5.30–9pm.

Shuaifu Restaurant $$ *19 Qianhai Beiyan, tel: 6618-5347/8.* An old-style restaurant featuring food that Marshal Nie Rongzhen used to serve at banquets; it was originally created by the famous military leader's chef. Open daily 5pm–11pm.

Sichuan Restaurant $$ *14 Liuyin Jie, Xicheng District, tel: 6615-6924.* A well-known restaurant serving excellent Sichuan food in the midst of the gardens of Prince Gong's Mansion, one of the best-preserved – and most elaborate – courtyard homes in the city. A memorable experience. Open daily 11am–2pm and 5–9pm.

Source $$ *14 Banchang Hutong, tel: 6400-3736.* This elegant courtyard Sichuan restaurant gets rave reviews from overseas visitors who love its refined setting and foreigner-friendly Sichuan cuisine. Open daily 11am–2pm, 5.30–10.30pm.

Yuelu (Wushan Luyu) **$$** *10 Lotus Lane (He Hua Shi Chang), tel: 6617-2696.* Splendid Hunanese food in a sleek setting that combines traditional with modern. Chinese readers will find interesting books on its wooden shelves while those seeking privacy can reserve private rooms upstairs. This restaurant was opened by local artist Fang Lijun. Open daily 11–2am.

WESTERN DISTRICTS (XICHENG, HAIDIAN)

Baijia Dazhaimen $$$ *Suzhou Lu, Haidian, tel: 6265-4186.* Located in the grounds of a Qing-dynasty mansion. Eat in one of many pavilions or pagodas. Open daily 11am–2pm and 5–9.30pm.

Cepe $$$$ *The Ritz-Carlton Beijing, 1 Jin Cheng Fang Street East, Financial Street, tel: 6601-6666.* Often voted Beijing's best Italian restaurant. Customers point to the trademark porcini mushrooms (grown in an in-house humidor) and the extensive wine list. An upmarket experience you might not expect in Beijing. Open daily 11.30am–2.30pm, 6–10.30pm.

Golden Peacock Dai Ethnic Flavour $–$$ *16 Minzu Daxue Beilu, Weigongcun, Haidian, tel: 6893-2030.* Good hearty Dai ethnic food for almost nothing. This place is very popular, so you may have to wait for a table. Try their pineapple rice – the fruit is hollowed out and filled with sticky purple grains. The fish is also great, as are the deep-fried bananas. Open daily 11am–10pm.

Li Family Restaurant (Li Jia Cai) **$$$$** *11 Yangfang Hutong, Deshengmennei Dajie, Xicheng District, tel: 6618-0107.* Set in the humble rooms of a typical courtyard house located deep in a *hutong* neighbourhood, this is Beijing's most popular restaurant with visitors, requiring advance bookings. The recipes – created for the Qing Dynasty Empress Dowager – employ fresh, simple countryside ingredients prepared in the home kitchen. Flavours are odd and rustic; the Li version of Beijing duck is neither crispy nor oily. Open daily 6–8pm. No credit cards.

Nishimura $$$$ *Shangri-La Beijing Hotel, Level 2, 29 Zizhuyuan Lu, Haidian District, tel: 6841-2211, ext. 2719.* Beijing's first Japanese *robatayaki* (grill) restaurant also includes a takeaway counter and two *teppanyaki* counters, but the long grill is the place to sit. Order any item from the counter and the chef will grill it to perfection. The bacon roll with asparagus, a potato with butter, and the giant prawn are divine. Come at lunchtime for cheaper fare. Open daily 11.30am–2.30pm and 6–10pm.

Whampoa Club $$$$ *23a Jinrongjie, Financial Street, tel: 8808-8828.* Beijing's classiest designer restaurant – anyone who's got the money is dining here. Acclaimed chef Jereme Leung's Beijing food is not cheap but is very highly rated. Adding a funky touch are the black décor and suspended fish pond. Open daily 11.30am–10pm.

SOUTHERN DISTRICTS (XUANWU, CHONGWEN)

Gongdelin $$ *2 Qianmen Dongdaijie, Chongwen District, tel: 6702-0867*. With Beijing's most comprehensive vegetarian menu, the government-run Gongdelin turns out delicious dishes despite its ugly institutional interior. Entrées taste and look like popular Chinese dishes, and are usually made with pork, duck, chicken or fish. There's even a vegetarian Beijing duck *(suyazi)*. Open daily 10.30am–9.30pm.

Quanjude Kaoyadian $$$ *32 Qianmen Dajie, Chongwen District, tel: 6701-1379*. The Quanjude chain's most elegant Beijing duck restaurant enjoys its reputation for serving the best roast duck in the world. Dining rooms come in a variety of sizes; all are ornately imperial. Best appreciated as a banquet with four or more diners. Open daily 11am–2pm and 5–9pm.

WESTERN HILLS

Huangye Cun $$$ *Xiangshan Botanical Gardens, tel: 8259-9121*. Beautifully positioned in the grounds of the Botanical Gardens, this restaurant specialises in Shaoxing cuisine from southern China. Open daily 10.30am–9pm.

Songlin Restaurant $$ *Xiangshan Villa, east gate of Fragrant Hills Park, tel: 6259-1296*. This is a massive restaurant specialising in home-style cooking from Shandong province. There is the option of 'fast food' service or full restaurant facilities. Open daily 10am–4pm.

GREAT WALL

Badaling Restaurant $$$ *Badaling Great Wall, tel: 6912-1486*. This is the main state-owned restaurant at Badaling and the only one the tourist office will promote to groups. It can hold up to 1,000 people and serves Sichuan and Jiangsu food. Open daily 10am–3pm.

Simatai Restaurant $ *Simatai Great Wall, 98 Jingqu Lu, tel: 6903-5311*. Serves home-style food prepared by a Sichuanese chef with lengthy experience of working in Beijing. Open daily 8am–9pm.

INDEX

Berlitz pocket guide

Beijing

Third Edition 2008

Written by J.D. Brown
Updated by Dinah Gardner
Edited by Alex Knights and Caroline Radula Scott
Series Editor: Tony Halliday

Photography credits
Richard Nowitz except for: Ming Tang-Evans pp. 12, 51, 53; J.D. Brown pp. 24, 36, 54, 57, 65; Marcus Wilson-Smith pp. 18, 40, 55, 58, 66, 76, 87; Nicholas Sumner p. 41; Lance Dawning p. 64; Imagine China p. 79

Cover picture: Corbis

Printed in Singapore by Insight Print Services (Pte) Ltd, 38 Joo Koon Road, Singapore 628990. Tel: (65) 6865-1600. Fax: (65) 6861-6438

Berlitz Trademark Reg. U.S. Patent Office and other countries. Marca Registrada

Every effort has been made to provide accurate information in this publication, but changes are inevitable. The publisher cannot be responsible for any resulting loss, inconvenience or injury.

Contact us

At Berlitz we strive to keep our guides as accurate and up to date as possible, but if you find anything that has changed, or if you have any suggestions on ways to improve this guide, then we would be delighted to hear from you.

Berlitz Publishing, PO Box 7910, London SE1 1WE, England.
fax: (44) 20 7403 0290
email: berlitz@apaguide.co.uk
www.berlitzpublishing.com